Bismarck

ABOUT THE AUTHOR

Volker Ullrich is a German historian, journalist and author whose previous books include biographies of Napoleon and Hitler and a major study of Imperial Germany. From 1990 to 2009, Ullrich was the political books editor of *Die Zeit*.

Bismarck

The Iron Chancellor

Volker Ullrich

Foreword by Prince Ferdinand von Bismarck

Translated by Timothy Beech

HAUS PUBLISHING • LONDON

First published in Great Britain in 2008 by

Haus Publishing Limited
4 Cinnamon Row
London SW11 3TW

This second edition first published in 2021

Originally published under the title *Otto Von Bismarck*
in the 'rowohlts monographien' series
Copyright 1998 by Rowohlt Taschenbuch Verlag GmbH, Reinbek bei Hamburg

English translation copyright © Timothy Beech 2008

A CIP catalogue record for this book is available from the British Library

ISBN 978-1-913368-37-1
eISBN 978-1-913368-38-8

Typeset in Garamond by MacGuru Ltd

Printed in the United Kingdom

Front cover image courtesy akg-images

www.hauspublishing.com

Contents

Foreword by Prince Ferdinand von Bismarck

Bismarck was neither the creator of German unity nor the founder of the German Reich, but it was he who re-established both. It is crucially important to acknowledge this political as well as historical conclusion in order to counteract the prejudice that Germany is the 'youngest' and 'too lately established' nation in Europe. Following the period of mass migration, the German people, together with the French, were the oldest people in Europe. Around AD 900, it had already achieved its political as well as national unity. Bismarck said on 24 February 1867:

> There was a time when the German Reich was powerful, great and honoured because it was united and led by a strong hand. Its head and limbs share the responsibility for this Reich sinking into a state of disunity and impotence. However, the longing of the German people for their lost possessions has never ceased. The history of our time is the history of endeavours to win back for Germany and the German people their past glory!

Bismarck was determined to satisfy this longing. This aim was his life's work and it is almost incredible that he achieved it in such a short time.

Due to his innate sensitivity, he realised the Germans' longing for their lost unity at an early stage. As Bismarck was, like Goethe, a man of both thought and action, his open declaration in the Reichstag on 9 July 1879 did not really surprise anyone:

From the very beginning of my career I have had only this one guiding star: by which way and means could I lead Germany into unity and in so far this was achieved, how could I strengthen and support this unity and finally make it a result of the free will of all its participants?

He made it his task to re-establish the unity of the Germans that had been lost for centuries, and his ability to do so was due to his energy, sensibility, literary education and expressiveness. His extensive knowledge and his pragmatic understanding of history were requirements for his well-considered, imaginative and, as far as possible, successful politics. According to the historian Ernst Engelberg, Bismarck 'grew to be a figure of historical importance whose understanding of the world and far-sightedness have ever since been fascinating his contemporaries as well as posterity'.

The German Reich founded by Bismarck is even today to be seen as the foundation, standard and legal basis of all German policy. His Reich was an important and strong country, but was at no point predominant amongst the European states. Bismarck set the benchmark for succeeding chancellors by demonstrating how, in the middle of Europe, German foreign and domestic policy could be turned into a policy of peace for the whole of Europe. His social policy was also a model for many countries.

In a statement in defence of his honour, the French ambassador in London at that time concluded: 'I am firmly convinced that as long as Bismarck is in control of the situation we can absolutely rely on German loyalty. But as soon as the chancellor resigns from his office, stormy times are going to come for Europe.'

Finally, it was Gustav Stresemann who said:

It would be good to write a book on the misunderstood Bismarck in which it is shown that he was the one who at the height of his power was actually the most careful in making use of it and how he asserted himself in 1866 and 1870 against those who could not get enough of it. He wanted to keep the peace in Europe. This would be a better image of him than the one generally created by legend which shows him as a man in cuirassier boots.

Prince Ferdinand von Bismarck
October 2007

Introduction

Those who possess great political power for a long time and then suddenly lose it generally feel the urge to compose their memoirs – not only in order to transmit to posterity as favourable a view as possible of their own achievement, but also so as to settle accounts with former political opponents. It was no different in the case of Otto von Bismarck after his fall. On 16 March 1890, one day after his definitive break with the young Kaiser Wilhelm II, he confided to a visitor: 'Now I am going to write my memoirs'.[1] Meanwhile, the Reich Chancellery was already piled high with boxes full of secret files that Bismarck, during the next few weeks, would have taken to Friedrichsruh, his place of retirement in the Saxon Forest, outside Hamburg.

As his assistant, Bismarck chose Lothar Bucher, a former 1848 liberal whom he had appointed a councillor in the Foreign Ministry, where he served Bismarck faithfully. Without Bucher's insistence, Bismarck's memoirs would probably never have been written.[2] The ex-chancellor was often lacking in enthusiasm. He was capable of spending hours stretched out on the chaise longue immersed in reading the papers while his amanuensis sat at the table, pencil ready, waiting to record his words. When the grumpy old man finally began dictating, his account of events would be selective and disordered, constantly mixing history with reflections on the political events of the day; as a result, Bucher became quite desperate. He complained in January 1892:

It is not just that his memory is defective and his interest in what we have already done is slight.

He actually tries to distort things deliberately, even when it comes to well-established facts and events. He will not admit to having been involved in anything that failed, and he will not allow that anyone other than himself made a contribution.[3]

It was Bucher's task to bring order to this chaotic material, correcting the most egregious errors, and to make a publishable text out of mere fragments. The final product was very far from complete in October 1892, when, in a hotel on Lake Geneva, Bucher died.

Up to his own death on 30 July 1898, Bismarck continually made small revisions to the already-completed sections, without taking the work any further. The first two volumes of his *Memories and Reflections* were published by Cotta at the end of November 1898; the third volume, centring on Wilhelm II and the events surrounding Bismarck's dismissal, only appeared in September 1921, after the end of the Wilhelmine Reich. It proved more successful than anyone had expected. 'In the bookshops,' noted Hildegard von Spitzemberg, 'people are coming to blows over Bismarck's memoirs ... The edition of 100,000 copies is long since out of print, and there is no way that Cotta can meet the continuing demand.'[4]

In his final years, Bismarck had become a living monument to himself, and his memoirs played no small part in exalting his historical importance into the realms of myth. They provided the orthodox view of Bismarck – which dominated German historiography up to 1945 – with an inexhaustible stock of quotations, and they shaped the image many patriotic Germans had of the founder of the first German nation state: 'Lesser German' but 'Greater Prussian'. For a long time, this made it more difficult to form a sober, undistorted view of this figure who had such a large impact on German history. Though the literary quality of many sections of Bismarck's memoirs still continues to impress, as a historical source they should be used only with the greatest caution.

The idolisation of Bismarck that predominated for so long was matched by a demonising view, the other side of the coin; as the journalist Maximilian Harden remarked critically as early as 1896, this tended to 'depict him as a pitch-black, diabolically clever Machiavellian caricature, occasionally dressing up on a whim as a sulphur-yellow cuirassier'.[5] After 1945, the inclination to paint Bismarck as the villain responsible for all the distortions of German history in the first half of the twentieth century was for a time very widespread, and even today such a view has some advocates.[6] Modern historians, however, have moved away equally from both the positive and the negative legends. There are now three important Bismarck biographies, each of which in its own way represents a significant historiographical achievement.

The first of these, by the Frankfurt historian Lothar Gall, appeared in 1980. He was the first to succeed, with aplomb, in navigating between the Scylla of Bismarck-worship and the Charybdis of demonising the German statesman, instead considering him critically within the terms of his own times. Gall sees Bismarck as someone with a great deal of influence on events who was nonetheless unable to control the changes he had unleashed, and as an arch-royalist who wanted to preserve Prussia's conservative political structures but who also did much to further the process of economic and social modernisation. In short, Bismarck was a 'white revolutionary' – Gall's subtitle was borrowed from an essay by Henry Kissinger – who, like the sorcerer's apprentice, ended up being unable to master the powers he had summoned.[7]

In 1985, the first volume of Ernst Engelberg's Bismarck biography appeared in a simultaneous edition published by the Akademie Verlag in East Berlin and the Siedler Verlag in West Berlin; at the time, it was rightly celebrated as a German achievement on both sides of the Wall. People were inevitably surprised at the way a leading East German historian, a Marxist, approached this figure, till now decried as the ultimate embodiment of reactionary 'Prussianism', with such understanding and at times even sympathy. It was quite possible to read the book as a cautious attempt at a return to a common national sense of shared traditions, reappropriating the 'historical heritage'. In a sense, this first volume anticipated the events that would have already occurred by the time the second volume appeared in 1990 – the collapse of the GDR and the unification of the two German states that had arisen from the bankrupt remains of the nation Bismarck had created, the German Reich.[8]

The chief difference between these two works and the great Bismarck trilogy by the American historian Otto Pflanze, completed in 1990, is that Pflanze's biography brings the great statesman's complex personality far more into the foreground. Pflanze has no hesitation in placing Bismarck on the couch, as it were, to consider him from a psychoanalytic point of view. In this way, he makes interesting findings about the relationship between Bismarck's nervous constitution and his political behaviour, among other things.[9] But the problem with this psychoanalytic approach is that it often amounts to little more than guesswork, because there are aspects of Bismarck's inner life that he kept hidden even from those closest to him. 'Faust complains of the two souls dwelling in his breast; but I play host to a whole bickering crowd of them. It is just like a republic', he confided to a friend. 'I pass on most of what they say. But there are entire provinces I will never open to the gaze of another human being.'[10] Even a psychoanalytically-trained historian will never be able to penetrate Bismarck's many-sided personality in all its aspects. For this reason, the following comment from 1910 remains true today: 'Like Frederick the Great and Goethe, Bismarck is a figure we will never get to the bottom of. Really, everyone makes their own biography of such men as these.'[11]

Early influences 1815–32

It is surprising how frequently Bismarck referred to his childhood and youth, even in old age, when he was the most successful politician in Europe. This need to speak of his early years derived from his conviction that 'no-one ever loses the impressions made on him by his youth'.[12] When the chancellor of the Reich looked back in this way, his memories were not exclusively affectionate.

Otto von Bismarck was born in Schönhausen near the Elbe on 1 April 1815 – the year when the usurper Napoleon was beaten for good and the European balance of power was restored at the Congress of Vienna under the banner of a monarchist revival. During the 'wars of liberation', many patriots had imagined the formation of a unified Germany, but what emerged instead was the German Confederation, a loose association of thirty-four individual states (and four free cities) under the domination of Austria and Prussia, the two leading powers in the region. This Austro-Prussian dualism was to persist until 1866, when Bismarck forcefully broke it up, permanently destroying the system of the German Confederation.

Bismarck's childhood was coloured by family tales about the period of French domination. His parents had been married for just a few months when French soldiers occupied Schönhausen after the defeat of Prussia at Jena and Auerstedt, plundering both village and manor. 'The Prussian state has been torn apart, and all that is Prussian by name has been insulted, and humiliated,' said Bismarck's paternal uncle, Friedrich von Bismarck, after the Peace of Tilsit in 1807,[13] which compelled Prussia to give up its territory west of the Elbe. It got these lands back in 1815, together with parts of Westphalia and the Rhine Province, but the Prussian territories were still not geographically unified; the western and eastern parts were divided by Hanover and Hesse. It was to be Bismarck's defining aim as a politician to bring this state of affairs to an end, increasing Prussia's power within Germany and developing its position in Europe.

The watershed of 1815 was a significant influence on Bismarck, but his unusual family background was still more important. His parents came from utterly different milieus. Bismarck's father, Karl Wilhelm Ferdinand von Bismarck, came from an old-established noble family of the Altmark that provided a steady succession of officers to its rulers in Brandenburg and subsequently Prussia, without particularly distinguishing itself in any other way. On the other hand, his mother, Wilhelmine Mencken, was from a family of scholars and high-ranking civil servants; her father, Anastasius Ludwig Mencken (1752–1801), had been appointed cabinet secretary by Frederick the Great, advancing under his successors to full cabinet membership and even briefly serving as head of the cabinet. It is not entirely clear why, in 1806, the daughter of this educated, worldly figure accepted the proposal of a country squire eighteen years her senior, but it seems her family pushed her gently in this direction.[14] The marriage did not turn out to be a happy one. Ferdinand von Bismarck may have been a good-humoured patriarch, in no way tyrannical, but as a member of the Prussian landed gentry his intellectual horizons were too limited for him to offer his wife's enquiring mind much in the way of stimulation. She withdrew more and more from her unsatisfying situation into preoccupation with illnesses and upsets. Decades later, Otto's cousin Hedwig, one of his childhood playmates, still remembered Bismarck's mother as having been 'often miserable and distracted': 'These days one comes across the word "nervous" in every quarter, but the first time I heard it applied – once I had grown up – was to this woman. It was generally said that through her nervous disposition she made things harder for herself, and harder still for her husband and children.'[15]

Otto von Bismarck was the fourth of six children; only three of them lived beyond infancy – his older brother, Bernhard (born in 1810), his younger sister, Malwine (born in 1827), and Bismarck himself. There has been much speculation as to whether he mostly took after his father or his mother. From his father he inherited his large, powerful stature, as well as his lifelong affinity with the world of the Prussian landed gentry. In a letter of March 1847 to his wife Johanna von Puttkamer, he wrote with great pride of the longstanding ascendancy of the conservative principle here in the 'house where my ancestors have for centuries been born, lived, and died in the same rooms'.[16] But Bismarck's mother had introduced an element into the family that put this unbroken relationship with his paternal inheritance in question. It was from her that he inherited his sharp intelligence and cool rationality, together with his sensitive feeling for language, a certain nervous instability and, above all, the insatiable ambition to escape from the narrow confines of the life of a Prussian country noble. The traits and inclinations he inherited from his ill-matched parents were contradictory indeed. This explains the uncertainties and hesitations of the young Bismarck, and it also illuminates some of the inconsistencies of his personality as a mature politician.

Bismarck passed his first years on the Kniephof estate in Pomerania; his father had acquired it on favourable terms in 1816 while still retaining the Schönhausen property. Kniephof, with its ancient oaks and beeches, its meadows and fishponds, was the paradise of Bismarck's boyhood, where he could roam free and wild to his heart's content. This was the origin of his love of the country, of trees and solitary forest walks. But this country idyll came to an abrupt end. At the beginning of 1822, Bismarck's mother, keen as she was on education – she envisaged a career in the civil service for both her sons – packed the six-year-old Otto off to the Plamann Anstalt in Berlin, the boarding school that his brother was already attending.

The unexpected transition to a wholly new life shaped by obligation and discipline was a shock for the boy, and even as an old man Bismarck harboured increasingly bitter memories of his time at boarding school. 'The Plamann Anstalt ruined my entire childhood', he would repeatedly complain. It was 'intolerably strict' and 'a false Sparta'. He was never able to eat his fill, he said, and he was continually exposed to 'rough treatment' at the hands of the teachers, who especially hated the sons of the aristocracy and woke them up in the morning 'with blows from their swords':

> The Plamann Anstalt was so situated that you could see out into the open country from one side; in those days the city came to an end at the south-west end of the Wilhelmstrasse. When I saw through the window a team of oxen pulling a plough, I would cry out of homesickness for Kniephof.[17]

Probably, the Plamann Anstalt was run on less strict and Spartan lines than the Prussian prime minister and chancellor of the German Reich later remembered. But Bismarck, used as he was to the freedom of life at Kniephof, evidently reacted more sharply to regimentation and control than the majority of his fellow pupils. His reluctance to recognise authority and subordinate himself to his superiors, which soon became apparent, seems to have first taken shape because of these experiences as a schoolboy.

He held his mother responsible for his unhappiness, feeling the lack of an emotional contribution on her part that would have represented a much-needed compensation for the travails of his life at school: 'She wanted me to study hard and make something of myself in the world, and it often seemed that she was hard and cold towards me; as a small child I hated her, and later I got the better of her through falsity and success'. In the same letter to his future wife, of 23 February 1847, in which, at the age of thirty-two, he made this remarkable admission about his troubled relationship with his mother – she had died of cancer on 1 January 1839, not yet fifty years old – he also said the following about his dealings with his father:

I truly loved my father, and when I was not with him, I felt remorse for my behaviour towards him, and made resolutions I did not keep to for long; for how often did I not repay his truly boundless, disinterested, good-humoured tenderness towards me with coldness and sulky manners? Still more often, so as not to depart from the outward form I felt was called for, I feigned love towards him when inside I was hard and loveless on account of apparent weaknesses it was not my place to judge and which only really vexed me when they were combined with disregard for correct form.[18]

These rather tortuous phrases make it clear enough what worried Bismarck in his father: the hearty, somewhat rough-and-ready manners of the Prussian landed gentry, so different from his mother's cultivated, correct manner. Bismarck's amiable but weak father could not serve as a role model, and, despite the hatred he felt towards his mother, it was her values he adopted, probably more than he himself was aware of.

Things became more bearable for the boy when, aged twelve and a half, he transferred to the gymnasium. According to one of his teachers at the time, 'Otto von Bismarck sat among his classmates with visible alertness, an open, friendly boy's face and shining eyes, bright as a button.'[19] This impression matches the famous portrait

Portrait of Bismarck in 1826 (aged eleven) by the Berlin court painter Franz Krüger.

of 1826 by the Berlin court painter Franz Krüger, which shows Bismarck in a jacket in the latest fashion, with a book wedged under his arm and, peeping out beneath his blond shock of hair, strikingly lively eyes with a slightly cheeky expression.

At the same time as moving to secondary school, Bismarck and his brother took up residence in a flat their parents maintained in Berlin. He was looked after by a housekeeper and received extra private tuition, and did what was required of him at school with a certain casualness. It seems he took advantage of many opportunities to skip lessons. His very last school report, under the heading 'Diligence', records: 'Not always consistent, and his attendance was irregular at times.'[20] Bismarck attended the Friedrich-Wilhelm Gymnasium in the Friedrichstrasse, then the Gymnasium zum Grauen Kloster in the Klosterstrasse, until taking the Abitur in 1832. During this period, Prussia's secondary schools were at the high point of a humanist revival, but it can hardly be maintained that this humanist education had much influence on Bismarck or left any lasting mark on his character. He soon came to the conclusion that Greek was completely pointless, though he remained convinced of the usefulness of reading Latin. This was his source for the aphorisms and quotations he was later to lard his speeches and letters with. However, according to the historian Erich Marcks, 'classical antiquity never became a living force for him, for all the memories and images that remained with him, either as a source of political and historical knowledge or as an aesthetic and ethical ideal'.[21]

The report on Bismarck's Abitur attested to the seventeen-year-old's 'very satisfactory ability' in German, and also that 'his performance in French and English was especially successful'.[22] His teachers thus recognised one of Bismarck's greatest gifts, his feeling for languages – not just his own, but foreign ones as well. He spoke English and French fluently and, during his time as ambassador in

St Petersburg, he was to master Russian in a short time. As far as the German language itself is concerned, it is probably no exaggeration to describe him as one of the most brilliant stylists of the century. As well as Bismarck's letters to his wife, many of his diplomatic essays and speeches – and some parts of his memoirs – are great literature, impressive for their powerful, elastic, transparent language and wealth of images drawn above all from country life. No German head of government since has ever equalled Bismarck in this respect.

Generations of schoolchildren knew the first sentence of Bismarck's memoirs by heart: 'A typical product of our state education, I left school in 1832 as a pantheist, and if I was not a republican, I certainly believed that a republic was the best form of government.'[23] But this view of Bismarck's, recorded sixty years later, was a conscious distortion calculated to blame the Prussian schools of the pre-1848 Vormärz period for excessive sympathy with enlightened and liberal ideas. Even when young, Bismarck was far removed from republican inclinations, and would remain so all his life. His words a few lines later were truer; he wrote that the influence of school had not succeeded in 'eradicating my innate Prussian and royalist sentiments – my historical sympathies remained on the side of authority'. Unconditional loyalty to the Prussian ruling house, unbroken fidelity to the traditions of aristocratic land ownership – these attitudes remained fundamental to all he thought and did.

'The Crazy Junker' 1832–47

On 10 May 1832, Bismarck entered 'Georgia Augusta', the University of Göttingen. After the calm of the 1820s, the times had once again become less politically settled. In July 1830, the system of the Restoration had received a nasty shock with the fall of the Bourbon dynasty in France, and revolutionary aftershocks could be felt throughout Europe. Even in some states within the German Confederation, there were disturbances and local revolts. At the end of May 1832, 30,000 German democrats gathered at Hambach Castle to demonstrate for freedom and German unity. Less than a year later, in April 1833, radical students stormed the Hauptwache in Frankfurt to make a gesture of protest against Metternich's repressive policy.

There is nothing to indicate that Bismarck, the newly matriculated 'studiosus of Law and Government Sciences' in Göttingen, was much affected by the political upheavals that followed the July Revolution in France. Phenomena such as the Hambach Fest and the Frankfurt putsch were highly disagreeable to him, as his memoirs record with (in this case) full credibility – 'tumultuous interference with civil order was at odds with my Prussian education'.[24] So it was no surprise that, rather than joining one of the student clubs suspected of revolutionary activities, he chose a patriotic Burschenschaft (fraternity), the Hannovera, whose members were mainly drawn from the families of Hanoverian officers and civil servants. Bismarck enjoyed its feuding, boozy life to the full, and later he would proudly recall that he had 'been in twenty-eight swordfights in three semesters, and always given a good account of himself'.[25] This towering, still-slender young man's extravagant outward manner was intentionally conspicuous – he wore a cloak resembling a dressing gown that came down to his feet, and he was accompanied by an enormous tawny dog.

This dandyish pose was matched by a tendency to grandiloquence; he apparently proclaimed to his Hannovera comrades, 'I will become either the greatest fool or the first man in Prussia'.[26] Of course, those who knew him well discovered another side to him beneath this reckless and inflated pose: a serious, reflective, well-read young man who could discuss history and literature with equal familiarity. A fellow student from America, John Lothrop Motley – who made friends with Bismarck in Göttingen and went with him when he left the university to study in Berlin in the autumn of 1833 – provided a psychological portrait of the young Bismarck in his autobiographical novel *Morton's Hope*, in which the character of Otto von Rabenmark appears: 'On the street and in the tavern he lives a wild life, but in his room he casts off the role of fool and starts talking sense.'[27]

However, Bismarck studied only in the most desultory manner. From term to term, the number of lectures he signed up for and attended grew steadily smaller. The only professor at Göttingen whose classes he regularly attended was the historian Arnold Heeren, who was already seventy-one. His views on the material and, above all, economic factors behind foreign policy and their influence on the development of the international system of states clearly had an influence on Bismarck, as well as provoking his disagreement. But he had nothing to do with Heeren's far-better-known colleague Friedrich Christoph Dahlmann, a liberal historian and political scientist, nor did he show much interest in the famous university figures of Berlin, for instance Friedrich Carl von Savigny, head of the Historische Rechtsschule ('Historical School of Law'). When his wife Johanna later remarked, on seeing the university building, 'You must have been there every day,' he is said to have 'quite wildly' answered, 'Never!'[28] Though this was one of Bismarck's characteristic exaggerations, it shows once again his dislike of academic scholarship. He limited his studies to the bare minimum, and he got what he needed for the exams by turning to a revision tutor, as was not unusual at the time.

In May 1835, Bismarck took his preliminary bar exam, and was then given the junior position of Auskultator at the Berlin City Court. Compared to his previous lifestyle, during these first months of his time as a junior civil servant he worked with application and discipline, but as early as the summer of 1835 slight doubts began to appear as to whether the career of a civil servant was for him. He wrote to Gustav Scharlach, a fraternity brother from Göttingen:

> I really don't believe that even the most perfect success, the longest title, and the biggest medal ribbon in Germany, the most amazing superiority will compensate me for the physically and spiritually shrunken breast that would result from such a life. I still quite often feel the inclination to swap my pen for a plough and my briefcase for a game bag – I will always have that to turn to.[29]

Two souls dwelt in his breast: his longing for the country, for an aristocratic existence – his paternal inheritance – and his striving for something higher, the unfolding of his latent intellectual capacities – his mother's legacy.

For the time being, he stuck with his decision to enter the diplomatic service after a normal apprenticeship in the administration. In January 1836, Bismarck petitioned the head of government in the Rhine Province, Adolf Heinrich Count von Arnim-Boitzenburg, for permission to take the examination needed to transfer from the legal to the administrative branch in Aachen. From April 1836, he composed the two essays required in the solitude of Schönhausen: an administrative piece entitled 'Economy in the state budget' and a philosophical essay on 'The nature and admissibility of oaths'. The oral exam at the end of June confirmed the result of the essays: 'Throughout, the candidate showed excellent judgement, rapidity in grasping the questions put to him and skill in verbal expression.'[30] Bismarck – 'very well suited' to the role – was appointed Referendar, the probationary first rung on the civil service ladder. Nothing further appeared to stand in the way of his career.

Bismarck had decided on Aachen because he hoped to complete his time as Referendar as quickly as possible there. Count Arnim-Boitezenburg recognised the unusual intelligence of the twenty-one-year-old and did everything he could to help him. He quickly rotated him through the various departments of the provincial administration. But once again, Bismarck was left unsatisfied by the bureaucratic daily round, hard though he tried to do what was expected of him. He sought out diversions and distractions, and Aachen, which at the time was a spa of international standing, had plenty of both to offer.

The Junker from Upper Pomerania found himself drawn to visitors from the English aristocracy, especially the ladies among them. In August 1836, just a few weeks after he took his oath as Referendar, he told his brother he had fallen in love, so deeply 'that it could not be sufficiently described by the boldest hyperboles of the Orient'.[31] The object of his devotion was called Laura Russell, and was introduced to him as the niece of the Duke and Duchess of Cumberland. By the end of September, he was boasting that they were 'as good as betrothed'.[32] It cost a lot of money to move in these sophisticated circles, more money at any rate than Bismarck had. He tried his luck at the gaming table, lost, and ended up even deeper in debt. Once, his father helped him out with the considerable sum of 200 Reichstaler, but his money troubles did not go away and, to Bismarck's dismay, the creditors appeared out of nowhere 'like night watchmen when the alarm is sounded'.[33] Bismarck's superior warned the bon vivant to take his professional duties more seriously. In January 1837, Bismarck was already boasting to his brother of a new amorous adventure, this time with a thirty-six-year-old French married woman – as he wrote, 'a femme de qualité ... very well preserved, a tasteful flirt'.[34] He was still playing the part of the show-off and behaving like an immature undergraduate. But in the summer of that year, things turned serious. Bismarck fell head-over-heels in love with another beautiful English girl, the seventeen-year-old Isabella Loraine-Smith, a friend of Laura's. Stretching a two-week leave into months, he followed her right across Germany, spending money liberally on lavish champagne dinners and losing large sums at the gaming tables. Finally, after the hopes he pinned on the liaison had been dashed, he went back to Aachen with his tail between his legs.

But Count Arnim-Boitezenburg's patience was at an end. He suggested Bismarck should 'transfer to the government of one of the original Prussian provinces in order to return to greater exertions in official business, as proved impossible for you amidst Aachen society'.[35] So it seemed that the career begun with such great expectations had come to an early end. In September 1837, Bismarck went 'home to Pomerania, [his] pockets empty and sick at heart'.[36] In December 1837, he made a renewed attempt to complete his interrupted training as a Referendar in the Potsdam administration but, after just a few months, he gave up, choosing instead to complete his one-year's military service.

It was during this period, at the end of summer 1838, that he decided to leave state service. His cousin Karoline von Bismarck-Bohlen had doubts about this step and reproached him, but he justified it to her on the grounds that he wanted to be more than a mere cog in the bureaucratic machine:

> A Prussian civil servant is like a member of an orchestra. Whether he plays the first violin or the triangle, he has to play out the fragment allotted to him, with no view of the whole or power to shape it, whatever he himself thinks. But I want to make music as I see fit, if I am to make music at all.[37]

These words became famous, and have been interpreted again and again as looking forward to what was to come, to Bismarck's dominant role in Prussian politics; in fact, as Lothar Gall remarked, it was 'more a grand gesture, a fascination with his own image'.[38] He did not mention the more important reason he had for leaving the service, namely – as he confessed ten years later to his bride, Johanna – 'the absolutely enormous debts' he had accumulated, and that he saw 'no other way of settling than by acquiring an independent fortune'.[39] What could be more obvious than to return to his father's lands and manage them as profitably as possible? The desire to take revenge on his unloved mother may also have unconsciously played a part; she had wanted to force him onto the treadmill of a civil servant's career. Her final illness – she died on 1 January 1839 – coincided with her son's change of direction. Having failed in professional terms, Bismarck now followed in his father's footsteps by administering his Pomeranian lands.

Otto Pflanze, agreeing with the psychologist Erik Erikson, has described the period from Bismarck's twenty-third birthday to his thirty-second – between 1838 and 1847 – as a 'psychosocial moratorium' in his development.[40] In fact, this period was filled by profound inner turmoil and barely manageable tensions. At first, Bismarck found that the independent life of a country aristocrat provided him with what he had been longing for. He was subject to no one, had no orders to follow, and could make his own decisions. Within a short time, he had acquired an extraordinary degree of knowledge about rational agricultural management. Within a few years, supported by his brother, Bernhard, he had both reformed his father's lands and paid off the majority of his own debts. Nonetheless, all this activity was not enough to satisfy him, and he increasingly complained of boredom and loneliness. He tried to ease his unhappiness through rakish boozing, wild hunts and other excesses that made him well-known throughout Upper Pomerania as 'the Crazy Junker'. In 1842 he set off on a long foreign journey, which was still unusual for people of his background; he visited England, France and Switzerland. For a time, he flirted with the idea of a trip to Asia, 'to bring a bit of variety into the decoration of my comedy, and smoke my cigars on the Ganges instead of the Rega.'[41]

In the spring of 1844, Bismarck's dissatisfaction with the life of a country Junker led him to take an unusual step – he applied once more to the Potsdam administration to resume his probationary service. This time he stood it just a few weeks. He was even more repelled than previously by the 'insipid papermill of our administration, like threshing spent straw' and the narrow-minded presumption of his superiors. 'Now I'm stuck here', he wrote to his Göttingen student friend Scharlach in a letter of 9 January 1845, summing up his situation, 'a bachelor, very solitary, twenty-nine years old, fit in body again, but pretty lethargic mentally, doing what has to be done efficiently but without much enthusiasm'.

> My only company consists of dogs, horses and country Junkers, and I enjoy some regard in the eyes of the latter because I can read writing easily, dress like a human being at all times, yet I can dress a piece of game with the accuracy of a butcher, I ride with composure and daring, I smoke terribly strong cigars and drink my guests under the table with friendly efficiency.[42]

He was released from this frustrating lack of perspective and human contact through a new association with a group of Pomeranian pietists that had formed around the owner of the Trieglaff estate, Adolf von Thadden. Bismarck was introduced to this circle by a school friend from his Berlin days, Moritz von Blankenburg, who was engaged to Marie von Thadden, one of the daughters of the patriarch of Trieglaff. It was above all to this young woman, whose charm included a striking mixture of piety and sensuality, that Bismarck felt himself irresistibly drawn. He revealed an incredible amount about himself to her during their very first conversation in February 1843, when he bemoaned his 'constant, rootless boredom and emptiness. How do you expect me to have faith', he countered Marie's gentle remonstrances, 'when I simply don't believe? Either the faith must enter me from outside, or arise within me independently of my action or desire.'[43]

Naturally, Marie's interest in the unhappy master of Kniephof went beyond concern for the fate of his soul; she for her part felt strongly drawn to the 'Upper Pomeranian Phoenix', who was considered within her circle 'the epitome of wildness and arrogance'.[44] 'His engaging personality touches me too deeply for me to believe entirely in his wild life, when I see him,' she confessed to the man to whom she was engaged.[45] She could not afford to become too aware of her feelings, though, because separation from her 'good Moritz' was out of the question. The relationship between Bismarck and Marie von Thadden was charged with the appeal of being socially prohibited, and at the same time overshadowed by the fact they both knew their wishes could not be fulfilled.

Because Marie could not have the man she loved, she pinned her hopes on leading him to one of her closest friends, Johanna von Puttkamer, an intimate correspondent of hers. She was the only child of the owner of the Reinfeld estate in deepest Upper Pomerania and, like Marie von Thadden, she was religious and worldly at the

Johanna von Bismarck (née Puttkamer).

same time; however, she was not particularly attractive, apart from her thick black hair and dark eyes, which concealed hidden fires. At the wedding of the Blankenburgs in October 1844, Johanna – then twenty – was chosen as Bismarck's table-neighbour, though she does not seem to have made any impression on him then. They grew closer during a joint trip to the Harz mountains in July and August 1846, organised by the Blankenburgs.

The decisive change only came with the sudden death of Marie von Thadden on 10 November 1846. She had nursed her mother when she fell ill during a fever epidemic, and thus caught the deadly infection herself. It was in Schönhausen that Bismarck was informed of Marie's mortal illness, having moved there after the death of his father in November 1845. He was obviously deeply shaken by the news. That was the moment, he confessed in his famous letter of 21 December 1846 proposing marriage to Johanna's father, 'when the first heartfelt prayer, without speculation as to its rationality' had poured forth from his heart.[46] Marie's death led Bismarck to turn in on himself and reflect. There has been much debate as to whether this can be seen as a religious awakening, a 'conversion', properly speaking. There is certainly room for doubt. Bismarck was never a literalistic believer, and he always took a stand against orthodoxy and the intolerance of the clergy. His relationship to God remained a very personal one. Just as he was later opposed to all doctrinaire principles as a politician, the historian Arnold Oskar Meyer wrote, 'his religious sentiments could not be confined in the chains of any rigid dogma or ecclesiastical prescriptions'.[47]

Bismarck now concentrated on winning Johanna's hand. His 'letter of proposal' to Heinrich von Puttkamer was meant to prepare the ground. Many of his biographers see indications in this letter of his subsequent diplomatic brilliance. Indeed, it was composed with such skill that it was almost impossible for Heinrich to turn Bismarck down out of hand. Bismarck was fully aware of the reservations the pious Puttkamers had about him – 'the Crazy Junker' – so he tried to give a credible demonstration of his change of heart in the form of a lengthy review including his parents' origins, his education and his religious development. The first sentences aim at pietist feeling. Bismarck admitted that his request 'for the most precious thing you have to grant on this earth' – Puttkamer's only daughter – demanded 'the strongest proof of trustworthiness', adding straight away that 'when so dear a gift is granted faith in God must perform that which faith in man alone cannot'.[48]

The reply was evasive; this bold proposal was too great a surprise for Johanna's parents. Bismarck then made directly for his goal. He went to Reinfeld on 12 January 1847 and 'by means of a decisive accolade' – that is, by embracing Johanna – 'as soon as I set eyes on her, moved things on to the next stage, to the complete astonishment of her parents, so that everything was sorted out for the best within five minutes'.[49] A diplomatic manoeuvre followed up by a surprise attack – this was to be a method Bismarck would turn to brilliant effect later, when he held political office. He told his brother the news proudly:

> Generally speaking, I think I have achieved great good fortune, and something I no longer hoped for, by marrying, to put it bluntly, a woman of unusual intelligence and unusual nobility of temperament; at the same time, she is utterly adorable and *facile à vivre* as no other woman I have ever known.

Facile à vivre – it is easy enough to see what Bismarck meant by this. In Johanna, he had found a woman prepared to accommodate his every wish, subordinate her own needs to his and provide what his mother had denied him: a stable emotional relationship. The letters they wrote to one another after their engagement are true human documents, deserving a place amongst the greatest epistolary literature of the nineteenth century. At first there were moments of strangeness, irritating misunderstandings. They differed in the strength of their religious feeling, and Bismarck strove to bring about an approximation of their views:

> How is it that you people generally have so little trust in your faith, and wrap it up in the cotton wool of seclusion, to prevent any breath of air from the world from cooling it? ... If everyone that believed they had discovered the truth thought like that ... what kind of Pennsylvanian prison would God's beautiful earth become, divided into thousands upon thousands of exclusive coteries by insurmountable shibboleths?[50]

In this loving epistolary dialogue, Bismarck was the one who warned and made demands. Though he repeatedly criticised his own patronising tone, his aim was to shape Johanna according to his own image. She should learn to ride, and learn French too, so she could play the part of a diplomat's wife. The wedding took place on 28 July 1847. The marriage, which lasted over four decades and produced three children – Marie (1848), Herbert (1849) and Wilhelm (1852) – was happy, because Johanna devoted herself entirely to caring for her husband and children, sacrificing all desires of her own.[51] She was the stable point in Bismarck's life, the centre he needed to find his inner balance. 'You are my anchor on the sheltered bank of the river', he once wrote in the early years of their marriage. 'If it should come adrift, may God have mercy on my soul.'[52] Now that Bismarck had found secure moorings in his personal life, he could turn to his true passion – politics.

Bismarck's path to politics 1847–51

Friedrich Wilhelm IV was crowned King of Prussia on 15 October 1840. Bismarck attended the celebrations in the Lustgarten at the Berliner Schloss with his father. After decades of stagnation, with this new reign Prussian politics seemed to have come back to life again. The liberals hoped the new king would introduce overdue reforms, in particular the constitution that had been promised in 1815. They were soon disappointed. Friedrich Wilhelm IV believed quite literally that he reigned by divine right, and he inevitably saw the demand for a constitution as a direct attack on his role as monarch. The single concession he was prepared to make was to summon the Vereinigter Landtag, a legislative assembly drawn from members of the eight provincial assemblies, at the beginning of February 1847. The liberals were naturally not going to be satisfied with that. For Bismarck, however, the negotiations in the Vereinigter Landtag during the spring and summer of 1847 served as an opportunity to launch a vertiginous political career.

During his early years as a country Junker at Kniephof, Bismarck had already taken his first modest steps in the political arena. He had been a deputy in the local district administration of Naugard, and in this capacity he had sometimes stood in for his brother, Bernhard, in local parliamentary business. From late 1843 onwards, his involvement with the pietist circle of Adolf von Thadden had brought him into closer contact with influential conservative politicians, particularly Ludwig von Gerlach, president of the Magdeburg

Court of Appeal,[53] whose brother, Leopold von Gerlach, was one of the king's closest advisers. Bismarck had doubtless thought that the patronage of the Gerlach brothers could be advantageous to him, and it was above all in order to cultivate this political connection that he had leased Kniephof in 1845 and moved to Schönhausen, near Magdeburg. It was there that he had been appointed superintendent of the dykes on the Elbe in the late autumn of 1846, his first public post. Shoulder to shoulder with Ludwig von Gerlach, he had fought for the retention of an ancient privilege of the local aristocracy, *Patrimonialgerichtsbarkeit*, or jurisdiction over minor legal matters within their estates. It was with the conscious intention of defending conservative class interests against all demands made against them in the prevailing liberal atmosphere that, in May 1847, Bismarck took up his own mandate in the Vereinigter Landtag, replacing a member of the Provincial Parliament of Saxony prevented from attending by illness.

In his very first speech on 17 May 1847, the thirty-two-year-old newcomer from the provinces took an arch-royalist position, attacking the liberal interpretation of the popular movement of 1813 and the demands for a constitution that rested on this. At the time, he argued, the only issue had been liberation from Napoleon's foreign dominion – not liberal demands:

> In my view, it does no service to national honour to assume that the mistreatment and humiliation that the Prussians suffered under a foreign despot were not in themselves enough to make their blood boil, their hatred for the interlopers insufficient to overshadow all other feelings.[54]

As he reported to Reinfeld the next day, the expression of these views provoked 'an unprecedented storm of displeasure'.[55] Bismarck's reaction to this storm was notably cool; he turned his back on the assembly, took a newspaper out of his coat pocket and read it until the upheaval had subsided.

To liberal ears, Bismarck's remarks in his speech on the 'Jewish question' on 15 June 1847 were also highly provocative. His position was one of brusque opposition to the full political emancipation of Jewish people, particularly their demand 'to take on a role in government in a Christian state; for if I imagine being obliged to obey a Jew as a representative of the sacred majesty of the King, I have to confess that I would feel deeply oppressed and humiliated'.[56] After this speech, he wrote to his wife that he 'stopped walking down the Königsstrasse in the evening, because the Jews cut me dead'.[57] For Bismarck, the liberal advocates of Jewish emancipation were 'idiotic bores droning on about humanity'. Like the majority of his conservative fellow aristocrats, he had many anti-semitic prejudices, and this was not altered by the fact that later, as prime minister, he chose a Jewish banker, Gerson von Bleichröder, to administer his property.[58]

During the two months that the Vereinigter Landtag sat, Bismarck felt intoxicated – 'this business is much more interesting than I thought it would be'.[59] In politics, he had finally found an arena that he saw corresponded to his talents, and which he would now never be able to leave. Passionately – 'in an uninterrupted state of excitement that barely allows me to eat and sleep' – he joined the fray. By the end of the session, he had achieved his aim: he had made a name for himself as an uncompromising ally of the crown, extended his influence among the ultraconservative circles of the court party, and made a positive impression on the king himself. The prospects for Bismarck's political future seemed to be dazzling.

But then the March Revolution of 1848 threatened to undo everything Bismarck had achieved. Once again, the impulse came from France, but this time, unlike in 1830, the two leading German powers were also caught up in the revolutionary tide. On the night of 13 March, Klemens von Metternich, the symbol of the Restoration, was forced to flee Vienna; on 18 March the revolution was also victorious in Berlin, after bloody fighting on the streets. 'Alas, my soul is mortally troubled! ... We stand at the gates of the Republic,' lamented the Prussian Major Albrecht von Roon, an acquaintance of Bismarck's from the Pomeranian circle.[60] A day later, Friedrich Wilhelm IV was compelled to bow before the victims of the barricades piled up in the Schlosshof, and on 21 March the sovereign rode through Berlin wearing a black-red-and-gold armband. He announced that Prussia would now merge into Germany.

On the same day, Bismarck was in Potsdam to sound out the military on possible counter-action. On hearing that revolution had broken out, he had gathered together the farmers loyal to the king and armed them with shotguns; he was seriously thinking of coming to the aid of the king, whom he suspected to be in the custody of the revolutionaries, with this force. But in Potsdam General von Prittwitz, commander of the armed forces, indicated to him that he had no need of the support of an undisciplined band of peasants – it would be more useful for Bismarck 'to send potatoes and grain'.[61] But Bismarck continued to scheme. On 23 March he managed to speak to Princess Augusta, the wife of the king's brother Prince Wilhelm, who had fled to England the day before. He tried to gain her support for his plan for a counter-revolution that would replace the reigning monarch with her absent husband. Augusta rejected the idea on the spot. Whatever the details of this remarkable interview may have been – the later accounts of Augusta and Bismarck are very different[62] – it left Augusta, the future Prussian queen and empress of Germany, with a passionate hatred for the Junker from Schönhausen, who she felt had been intransigent and disloyal. Even in old age, Bismarck complained that she had always placed obstacles in his path and 'indeed caused more problems than all the foreign powers and opposing parties at home'.[63]

On 25 March, Bismarck was forced to bury his hopes of turning the clock back by force. Before his corps of officers in Potsdam, Friedrich Wilhelm IV averred that he had never felt safer or more at liberty than when he had been under the protection of his loyal Berlin citizenry. 'It was with a feeling of shock that I went back to Schönhausen', Bismarck recalled.[64] For a time he probably thought of making his peace with the new situation. At any rate, in a speech to the newly assembled Vereinigter Landtag on 2 April 1848, his tone was strikingly moderate. He offered to collaborate with the March ministry, controlled by Ludolf Camphausen and David Hansemann, the leaders of the Rhenish liberal opposition. Bismarck added, 'The past is buried, and I regret more keenly than many of you that there is no human power capable of reawakening it now that the Crown itself has thrown earth on its own coffin'.[65]

Among his ultraconservative friends and supporters, this apparent change of heart provoked outrage. He told his wife on 3 April that Ludwig von Gerlach and Adolf von Thadden had visited him 'to carry out the executioner's duty'.[66] Three months later, at the beginning of July 1848, when the wind had changed and counter-revolution was on the ascendant throughout Europe, Bismarck formally apologised to Ludwig von Gerlach for his earlier vacilla-tion: 'I have never reproached myself more for anything I did ... It can't be undone, but I have learned my lesson'.[67]

After months of forced inactivity, from the summer of 1848 Bismarck was once again entirely in his element. He played an enthusiastic part in setting up the ultraconservative *Neue Preussische Zeitung* ('new Prussian newspaper') – which soon became known as the *Kreuzzeitung* ('cross newspaper') on account of the Iron Cross that appeared as a vignette in the masthead – and even wrote the odd article, though generally without signing his name. At the same time, he helped to support the material interests of landown-ers east of the Elbe. In August 1848, 400 landed gentry met in a

'Junker parliament' to protest against any threat to property, and this happened to a considerable extent on Bismarck's initiative.

When Robert von Keudell, a friend of the Bismarck family, saw the thirty-two-year-old Bismarck again at this time, he was shocked by the change in his appearance, describing 'the seriousness and worry in his frowning features, his thinning head of hair; he seemed ... to have aged many years.'[68] This was the price Bismarck had to pay for his feverish political activity. There was scarcely anyone who was so busy in the second half of 1848; looking back, he wrote that he had 'gone back and forth' between Schönhausen, Berlin, Potsdam and Brandenburg 'like a pendulum, and I never want to see the Genthiner Chaussee ever again'.[69] His silent services came to be appreciated in the circle of the Kamarilla, the secret opposition 'shadow government' at the Berlin court. Ludwig von Gerlach called him the 'now very active and intelligent adjutant of our Kamarilla headquarters'.[70]

This activity bore fruit. By the early autumn of 1848, the position of the Prussian Crown was already so much strengthened, and that of the Berlin National Assembly and its appendage in Frankfurt so far weakened, that a coup was becoming ever more likely. At the end of October 1848, troops under the command of Prince Windisch-Grätz put down the rebellious citizenry of Vienna. Robert Blum, the envoy of the Frankfurt National Assembly, was summarily executed. Bismarck defended this bloody act to the Saxon diplomat Friedrich Ferdinand von Beust in frank terms: 'If I have an enemy in my power, I must destroy him!'[71] This was to remain his maxim later on, at least as far as domestic politics was concerned.

At the beginning of November 1848, counter-revolution was also victorious in Prussia. A new cabinet was appointed under Count Brandenburg, and the Berlin National Assembly was removed to Brandenburg and shortly thereafter dissolved. On 10 November 1848, General von Wrangel entered Berlin with his troops. In a letter in mid-November, Bismarck expressed his satisfaction to Johanna, writing, 'Politically speaking, everything has so far gone very much as I wished, and I am truly thankful to God that He has found me worthy to do considerable service on more than one occasion to the cause of right'.[72] Nonetheless Friedrich Wilhelm IV had not yet managed to make up his mind to give Bismarck a ministerial post as reward for these services. In the margin of a list of suggested names that included Bismarck's, the king noted, 'Only serviceable where the bayonet reigns supreme.'[73] Bismarck's reputation was that of a ruthless, reactionary agitator. This negative image continued to be a disadvantage in January 1849, when he had himself put forward as a candidate for the Second Chamber, which, according to the constitution published by the king on 5 December 1848, was to be elected on the basis of a more or less equal, but indirect, franchise.

Bismarck won his seat with a small majority, but after just a few months the king dissolved the Landtag and instituted the three-class franchise system that was to remain in force in Prussia until 1918. At the end of July 1849, Bismarck once again found a place in the newly elected chamber of the Landtag as a prominent advocate of the ultraconservatives. He had now decided once and for all to dedicate himself to politics. After he was re-elected, he let out Schönhausen and moved into a small flat in Berlin with his family. During the short session of the Second Chamber in the spring of 1849, an event occurred that was to be of great importance for Bismarck's future development as a politician. On 3 April 1849, Friedrich Wilhelm IV refused the imperial crown that was offered to him by a resolution of the Frankfurt National Assembly under its president Eduard von Simson. He did not want to be a king by the will of the people or wear a crown tainted by the 'mean stench of the revolution'.

But this did not mean the 'German question' had gone away. On the contrary, it was now 'on everyone's mind', as Bismarck was dismayed to note.[74] In a speech he made to the Second Chamber on 21 April 1849, Bismarck took the opportunity to defend the rejection of the imperial crown and thereby the Frankfurt Imperial Constitution:

> The crown of Frankfurt may shine brightly, but the gold that gives true value to its brilliance can only be obtained by melting down the Prussian crown, and given the form of this constitution I have no confidence that such a procedure would succeed.[75]

For Bismarck, it was out of the question for Prussia to be swallowed up by Germany. 'We are Prussians and Prussians we shall remain', he had pronounced to the editor-in-chief of the *Kreuzzeitung*, Hermann Wagener, at the beginning of June 1848, and this was to remain his view.[76] For him, what really counted was the preservation and growth of Prussian power. Next to this aim, nationalist sentiments definitely took second place, if he admitted their importance at all, and in August 1849 Bismarck cuttingly distanced himself from all politicians who believed the German question could be resolved by strong rhetoric and pithy resolutions:

> This question will be decided through diplomacy and on the battlefield, not in our assemblies, and all our talk and resolutions are no better than the moonshine musings of a dreamy boy building castles in the air who believes that something will come out of the blue and make him into a great man.[77]

Because he thought it was unrealistic and contrary to Prussian interests, Bismarck was also opposed to the idea of a 'union' – that is, the attempt the king and his advisers made shortly after the rejection of the Frankfurt Delegation to bring about a federal solution to the German question from above, without Austria and against her, by mutual agreement between the German princes. This would mean sacrificing the independence of Prussia on the altar of nationalist fantasies, Bismarck warned, as well as letting in by the back door the Frankfurt liberals they had just shaken off: 'We all want to see the Prussian Eagle spreading its wings from the Memel to the Donnersberg, to protect and to rule, but free it must be.'[78]

Bismarck also defended this position as a member of the Union Parliament that sat in Erfurt from 20 March 1850, which was supposed to advise on the constitution of the planned federal state. Much to his annoyance, Bismarck was chosen as secretary to Eduard von Simson, the president of the assembly: 'My dear departed father would turn in his grave if he heard I had become the secretary of a Jewish scholar.'[79] In a speech on 15 April 1850, he once again took a firm stand against the mediatisation of Prussia; should it ever happen 'that we dress the body of German unity in the threadbare coat of a French constitution', he argued, this must not lead to Prussia becoming the vassal of small and medium-sized states.[80]

An eyewitness description of Bismarck's appearance as a speaker has come to us from the short period of the Erfurt parliament:

> A tall, taut, rather rigid form with a blond beard and, though still young, a somewhat scanty head of hair rises up. It is the Junker of Bismarck-Schönhausen; a Junker, indeed, of the old style such as one seldom sees these days. He does not speak fluently, but rather forces the words out as though restraining his anger with the revolution and the revolutionary assembly in which he finds himself.[81]

This jerky, tentative manner of speaking, together with the rather thin, reedy voice that made a remarkable contrast to the massive form, were to remain characteristic of Bismarck as an orator. But when he made to speak he was met with tense expectation, and even his bitterest opponents paid him careful attention. Above all, it was his colourful and apophthegmatic language, peppered with sarcasm and provocative phrases, that held his listeners spellbound. Though he was opposed to parliamentarians and the parliamentary principle, Bismarck became one of the foremost parliamentary orators of his time.

As Bismarck had predicted early on, the project for a union failed. In April 1850 the Prussian plans were torpedoed by Austria, which had recovered its strength. Austria invited the governments of the individual states to Frankfurt to consult on restoring the German Confederation. After major conflicts between Vienna and Berlin that nearly came to war in the autumn of 1850, Prussia was forced to make the humiliating declaration, in the Punctation of Olmütz of 29 November 1850, that she was abandoning the union and was ready to return to Frankfurt without receiving any assurance from Austria of parity in the leadership of the German Confederation. The Prussian public, and many within the ranks of the conservatives, felt this agreement to be a humiliation. In a speech before the Second Chamber on 3 December 1850, Bismarck took it upon himself to defend the Punctation of Olmütz. He rose to this challenge with a bravura performance in which he conjured up the alternative to Olmütz, namely a Europe-wide war, in lurid colours, going on to stress the single principle that he thought should be of prime importance in taking any decision for peace or war:

The single solid foundation of a great state, and the thing that makes it essentially different from a small state, is national self-interest, not romanticism, and it is unworthy of a great state to fight for something that is not in its own interest.

This unashamed avowal of national self-interest as the driving force of foreign policy was a sign of Bismarck's readiness to outgrow his earlier status as a diehard defender of the interests of the Junkers alone. The speech, of course, included many things pleasing to the ears of his ultraconservative friends, for instance his concluding cry, 'I see the source of Prussian honour in Prussia keeping her distance from any shameful ties to democracy'.[82] This carefully calculated balancing act between realpolitik and a politics of conservative ideals was intended to make the thirty-five-year-old member of parliament seem a good prospect to the king and his Kamarilla for further employment in the diplomatic service, which had after all been his aim when he was a Referendar. At the end of April 1851, Bismarck was indeed appointed Prussian envoy to the Bundestag in Frankfurt – 'currently our most important diplomatic post', as he proudly reported to his wife.[83] This appointment caused something of a stir, because Bismarck had been so pointedly preferred to diplomats with many years' experience when he himself, in the words of Ludwig von Gerlach, 'had got no further in the civil service than to be a dissolute Referendar'.[84] The newcomer was to learn the diplomatic craft with extraordinary rapidity.

Diplomatic apprenticeship 1851–62

After just a week, Bismarck had already formed a definite opinion about the diplomats in Frankfurt. He wrote to Johanna:

> I have never had any doubt that they all cook with water; but I am surprised at such a thin, poor, watery soup without so much as a shimmer of mutton fat to be seen. Nobody, not even the most malicious democratic doubter, would believe the amount of fakery and self-importance there is in this diplomacy.[85]

Coming from a late entrant to the diplomatic trade, these were strong words; probably this exaggerated show of confidence concealed a degree of uncertainty felt by the Prussian country Junker regarding the part he himself had to play on this unfamiliar territory. Yet Bismarck's dismissive judgement did not lack justification; the frenzied activity of the representatives of the small and medium-sized states at the Bundestag mostly bore no relation to their actual political significance.

Bismarck came to Frankfurt having resolved to do his utmost to further Prussian interests, and above all this meant disputing Austria's claim to leadership within the German Confederation. Before 1848, the two great powers of Germany had maintained the balance of political power by exercising joint leadership, agreeing on the most important decisions in advance. In the reactivated German Confederation of 1850, however, the intention of Austria's prime minister

Prince Felix of Schwarzenburg was that Austria as presiding power really should play the leading role, leaving Prussia to be the junior partner. This was just what Bismarck was not prepared to accept. It was his aim to compel Austria to recognise Prussia's equal status within the German Confederation. The enduring dispute in which he became embroiled with the Austrian emissary, Count Friedrich von Thun, and his successors Anton Freiherr Prokesch von Osten and Johann Bernhard Count von Rechberg, arose from this stark difference of political interests.

In this, Bismarck was acting on the instructions of the Berlin government, but the manner in which he conducted the dispute in Frankfurt he largely determined himself. He seized every available opportunity to attack the Viennese diplomatic position and point out the limits of the Confederation's competence in Frankfurt. This extended to petty frictions over minor matters of protocol; the Prussian envoy did not shrink from a 'policy of harassment'[86] in order to hamper the work of the Bundestag and sometimes to bring it to a complete standstill. As his opponent von Thun concluded by September 1851, Bismarck seemed to belong 'exclusively to that party which just has the specific interests of Prussia at heart, and has little confidence in what the Bundestag might achieve'.[87]

The Austrians, on the other hand, predominantly sought to use the Bundestag as an instrument to further their own policy of hegemony in Germany. One example of this was their attempt to gain entry to the Zollverien ('customs union'), dominated by Prussia, by expanding the competence of the Confederation, so as not to lose out on this economic link. During a conversation with Bismarck at the end of November 1851, von Thun declared that expanding the customs union south-eastwards would naturally strengthen the 'preponderant influence of Austria within Germany', but still, that was 'in the nature of things'. Bismarck dissented in no uncertain terms: a Prussia that renounced 'the inheritance of

Frederick the Great' and contented itself with the role of 'Austrian Arch-Chancellor' would have no standing in Europe, 'and before I recommended such a policy at home, the matter would have to be decided by the sword'.[88] In the words of the historian Arnold Oskar Meyer, a keen admirer of Bismarck, this conversation was the first moment the Prussian envoy 'introduced a slightly metallic tone';[89] that is, he was directly threatening war, not just the withdrawal of Prussia from the German Confederation. Without doubt, this exceeded his instructions.

Prussia was eventually victorious in the dispute over the customs union. Austria was palmed off in 1853 with a trade agreement, remaining outside the union when it was renewed a year later and expanded to include the Kingdom of Hanover. This decision did much to lay the ground for the subsequent unification of Germany under the leadership of Prussia, without Austria. In a letter of December 1853 to Leopold von Gerlach, Bismarck made a preliminary assessment of his diplomatic experiences in Frankfurt:

> The arena of our policy is Germany, through our geographical situation alone, and this is the arena Austria also believes it needs for itself; given the claims Austria makes, there is no room for both, so we can make no lasting accommodation. We breathe the air away from each other's mouths, so one must yield or 'be yielded' by the other; and till that moment we must be opponents. I believe this to be a fact ... impossible to ignore, however unwelcome it may be.[90]

This did not mean Bismarck thought a violent resolution of Austro-Prussian dualism was inevitable; for now, he envisaged the option of war only 'if they keep shutting their ears to reason in Vienna', that is, if they persisted with 'the current system of raping Prussia through the Confederation' – as Bismarck put it.[91] If, on the other hand, Austria accepted that Prussia had equal rights, then a 'reformed dualism' in which Germany would be divided into two spheres of influence seemed a perfectly plausible option to him.[92]

However, the prospect of cooperation with Austria slipped into the background during the Crimean War of 1853–6. From the outset, Bismarck strove to exploit this conflict between the Western powers, England and France (with Turkey), and Russia, in order to improve Prussia's position in relation to Austria: 'Great crises bring about the weather that can further Prussia's growth, if we take advantage of them fearlessly, perhaps even quite ruthlessly.'[93] In Berlin, though, there was no agreement as to the best course for foreign policy. Whereas the Kamarilla, led by the Gerlach brothers, remained under the spell of the idea of the Holy Alliance, current during the post-Napoleonic period, and urged joining with Russia, a group of moderate conservatives gathered around the *Preussischer Wochenblatt* newspaper, founded in 1851 – from which they took the name of Wochenblatt Party – supported an alliance with the Western powers. King Friedrich Wilhelm IV was torn between desire to keep his country neutral and fear of leading it into isolation.

In April 1854 the Prussian government, led by Otto Theodor Freiherr von Manteuffel, gave in to pressure from Vienna and renewed a treaty of mutual defence and assistance signed three years previously. Bismarck was absolutely furious; after all, he had incessantly warned 'against tying our trim and seaworthy frigate to the worm-eaten old battleship of Austria'.[94] The Austrian government immediately took advantage of this by sending an ultimatum to Russia that compelled the tsar to vacate the Danubian principalities, which were then occupied by Austrian troops. The Habsburg Monarchy did not formally enter the war against Russia, but through this action it put itself clearly on the side of the Western powers. This seemed too much to the Berlin government, where the advocates of a policy of strict neutrality now gained the upper hand. At the beginning of 1855, Bismarck brought off the first 'master stroke of his political cunning'[95] when he deflected a request from Austria for the mobilisation of the armed forces of the German Confederation. This plan was aimed against Russia, but it thus came to nothing. The Prussian envoy had now acquired diplomatic stature. He served as the spokesman for a clear majority of the small and medium-sized states in the Bundestag; they too objected strongly to being taken in tow by the policy decisions of Vienna.

The Crimean War ended in a severe defeat for Russia, and the Congress of Paris of 1856 imposed hard conditions on the tsar. Those in St Petersburg felt they had been contemptibly let down by Vienna. This meant that the informal Holy Alliance of the conservative powers Russia, Austria and Prussia was destroyed. The beneficiary of this was France under Napoleon III, which was now to enjoy a leading role within Europe for a decade. A number of letters and memoranda written to Manteuffel during the spring of 1856 make clear the lesson Bismarck drew from this course of events: in order to provide diplomatic cover for the settling of scores with Austria that he thought inevitable in the long term, he recommended a closer approach to the new leading power, France, as well as the cultivation of Prussia's traditionally good relations with Russia. During August 1855, when Bismarck had visited Paris for the Exposition Universelle, he had been presented to the French imperial couple for the first time, and had been favourably impressed by the 'unusual politeness' they showed him.[96] His political mentors the Gerlach brothers were not at all pleased by his trip to Paris, suspecting that what lay behind it was a secret sympathy on the part of their protégé for Bonapartism and its exponent Napoleon III, whom they saw as nothing less than the embodiment of the hated revolutionary principle.

In the spring of 1857, this difference of opinion regarding the France of Napoleon III and its place in Prussian politics sparked a bitter conflict between the ambassador to Frankfurt and his

Napoleon III in 1852, painted by Franz Winterhalter.

ultraconservative friends. To Leopold von Gerlach's assertion that Napoleon III was 'our natural enemy' and so must remain,[97] Bismarck retorted that for him the legitimacy of a ruler was a matter of secondary importance. When it came to foreign policy, what interested him was 'France, whoever may currently be at its head, as a piece – and an indispensable one at that – on the political chessboard.' Bismarck summed up his opposing view in a sentence: 'When it comes to foreign powers and persons, my sense of duty in the service of my country abroad does not allow for having likes and dislikes.'[98] This expressed the core of their differences; whereas the Gerlachs obstinately barricaded themselves behind the rampart of their conservative principles, the single guiding principle for Bismarck when it came to foreign policy was the interest of the Prussian state. The image of the chessboard, which he was subsequently to use again and again, makes clear his priority: to prevent ideological axioms from blocking certain squares on the board in advance, so removing them from the range of possible diplomatic combinations.

The distance that now arose between Bismarck and his former patrons was also related to the changed political situation in Berlin. In October 1857, Prince Wilhelm of Prussia had become regent for his brother, who had suffered a debilitating stroke. This led to a perceptible loss of influence for the ultraconservative Kamarilla, because Prince Wilhelm – not least owing to the influence of his wife Augusta – favoured the Wochenblatt Party, which advocated joining forces with the moderate Lesser German nationalist wing of the liberals. In November 1858, the Manteuffel government was replaced by a cabinet whose tone was set by liberal conservative representatives of the Wochenblatt Party. In the general election called at the same time, the liberals achieved a landslide victory in the Prussian parliament, forming a strong majority in the new chamber. A 'New Era' had begun. In a royal address on 8 November 1858, Prince Wilhelm promised that in future Prussia would seek to make 'moral conquests' in Germany.

As early as March 1858, Bismarck had written a memorandum to the Prince Regent in an attempt to gain a foothold within the new tendency; because of its considerable length, it was known as the 'Little Book of Herr von Bismarck'. It repeated his well-known prophecy that in the not-too-distant future Germany would have to fight Austria for hegemony in Germany, but it also now made a commitment, anticipating to a certain extent the policy of 'moral conquests', to Prussia's nationalist mission. He argued that there was no conflict in principle between the interest of Prussia and that of the liberal and middle class nationalist movement. On the contrary, 'There is nothing more truly German than the development of Prussia's own interests, properly understood.'[99] This was a surprising change of direction in the national question on the part of the Prussian envoy. Had he not declared to the Danish envoy to the Bundestag, Bernhard Ernst von Bülow, at the end of 1856 that he 'was no friend of cheery or nationalist politics and far too definitely a Prussian to distinguish in his feelings between Spaniards, Bavarians or Danes'?[100] Now that the New Era in Prussia was beginning, he showed his determination to put the forces of German nationalism at the service of the expansion of Prussian power.

But of course there was nothing Bismarck could do to prevent his being recalled from Frankfurt and transferred to St Petersburg – 'sidelined on the Neva', as he felt it.[101] Annoyed that his enemies 'had arranged everything so underhandedly',[102] Bismarck became ill – a reaction of his volatile nervous constitution that was to be seen again and again in the future when he suffered political setbacks. Leaving Frankfurt came as a blow to the Bismarcks; they had passed the happiest years of their marriage in the villa on the Bockenheim Landstrasse just outside the city gates. When Motley, Bismarck's old friend from his student days, visited him in July 1855, he described the sociable atmosphere at the villa in the following terms:

Everyone comes together here, old and young, grandparents, children, dogs, and people eat, drink, smoke, play the piano and shoot with pistols (the latter in the garden), all at the same time. In this house everything is on offer that can be eaten or drunk on this earth; stout, soda, beer, champagne, burgundy, or claret can be had at any time, and everyone is constantly smoking the finest Havana cigars.[103]

Things were a lot less comfortable in St Petersburg, where Bismarck arrived at the end of March 1859 after six days' hard travelling. Nonetheless, the three years he spent – with interruptions – at this important location for European diplomacy were instructive for him, because he was able to broaden and deepen the insights he had gained in Frankfurt into the interests of the individual powers. From his very first day, the Prussian envoy enjoyed great goodwill in Russian governmental circles and at the imperial court. Relations between the two countries were better than ever, whereas those between Russia and Austria were at their lowest ebb. 'People have no idea how badly the Austrians are doing down here', he wrote to his wife on 6 April 1859. 'Not even a mangy dog would take meat from their hands ... The hatred is limitless, and greater than anything I had suspected.'[104]

Bismarck's relations with the staff of the Prussian embassy started on a less relaxed footing, especially with the legation secretary Kurd von Schlözer, who resisted Bismarck's inclination to exploit his subordinates' capacity for work to the utmost and impose on their loyalty beyond the call of duty: 'I realise that we must be constantly on the alert, and keep showing our teeth, or else we will be lost with him. Squeeze out the lemon and throw it away, that's his policy.'[105] It was a novel experience for Bismarck to find that someone beneath him should meet him with confidence rather than simply submit to him, and clearly a useful one; the result was that the two men became closer and grew to respect one another. In the end, even Schlözer was barely able to resist Bismarck's fascination: 'He is politics incarnate. Everything in him is on the boil, pressing to be actively realised.'[106] But this admiration was combined with a fearful question. 'Is he right for Prussia? Are the Prussians right for him? This volcanic spirit bursting out into our constricted, narrow situation!'[107]

It was no longer a secret among those around Bismarck that his political ambitions were now directed at the highest political offices in Prussia, but from St Petersburg his influence on politics in Berlin was limited, however much he showered the new foreign minister, Alexander Count von Schleinitz, and the prince regent

– who ascended the throne as Wilhelm I after the death of Friedrich Wilhelm IV in January 1861 – with letters and memoranda. What was more, Bismarck's ambitions received a blow when his left leg became inflamed in the summer of 1859 and the symptoms were worsened by inappropriate medical treatment. 'I am in an utterly miserable state, completely broken, lame, extremely tense ... quite without enthusiasm or even thoughts, so weak and tired to the point of collapse' – that was how he returned to Berlin in August 1859.[108] He was more or less set to rights by taking the baths in Wiesbaden and Nauheim but, while making a stop on the way back at the estate of a friend in East Prussia, he came down with an inflammation of the lungs that kept him in his sickbed for months. When the worst was over, Johanna – who devotedly tended her gravely ill husband – wrote: 'If only he would give up everything to do with politics and diplomacy, if we went straight back to Schönhausen as soon as he was completely better, thinking of nothing but ourselves, our children, parents and our really true friends, I would be so happy.'[109]

But such a withdrawal into private life was out of the question for Bismarck, however enticing the idea may occasionally have seemed to him. The force with which his passion for politics had taken hold of him and the strength of his desire to obtain a position of power that would allow him to put his political ideas and goals into practice were too great. Since his return to St Petersburg in June 1860, he had been more or less in a state of expectation, and the sharper the conflict in Berlin between the government and the Landtag over the reform of the army became – increasingly revealing the New Era to be an illusion – the more certain Bismarck grew that he would soon be called upon. At the end of April 1862, the moment finally seemed to have come. He was summoned to Berlin, where he was treated as prime minister in waiting. But Wilhelm I could not quite bring himself to choose Bismarck, and so at the end of May 1862 Bismarck was sent for the time being to Paris as envoy. From the outset, the minister for war, Albrecht von Roon, his confidant and advance guard in Berlin, was sure that this was just a temporary step: 'We need a decisive and capable prime minister, a man who can act himself and stir others to do so.' [110] Roon thought this man was Bismarck.

In the Prussian embassy on the Quai d'Orsay in Paris, Bismarck felt 'like a rat in an empty barn'.[111] He had many personal conversations with Napoleon III and went to see the International Exhibition in London. While he was there, it appears he spoke quite plainly to the leader of the opposition, Benjamin Disraeli, about his intention to involve Austria in a war over hegemony in Germany. Disraeli is reported to have said afterwards, 'Take care of that man! He means what he says.'[112] The longer the expected news of his appointment was delayed, the more impatient Bismarck became. In the end, he requested a six-week leave of absence in order to recover from the excitements of the past months far removed from the capital and from political activity.

The fashionable spa of Biarritz at which the forty-seven-year-old Bismarck spent the whole of July turned out to be a fountain of youth. Bismarck bathed in the sea twice a day, enjoying the sun and the rich Atlantic air – and he fell passionately in love with Katharina Orloff, the attractive twenty-two-year-old wife of the Russian ambassador to Brussels, Nikolai Orloff. 'The most charming of all women', he enthused quite openly to his wife, 'and you will love her very much when you get to know her better; she is a chip off the old block of Marie Thadden ... funny, clever and charming, pretty and young'.[113]

Johanna's reaction was astoundingly generous:

If I had any inclination to envy and jealousy, I could probably now be tyrannised into the lowest depths of these passions. But my soul simply does not have the materials for it, and I am just constantly delighted that my dear husband has encountered this charming woman there. Without her company, he would never have managed to find peace in one spot for so long, and he would not have become so well, as he boasts in every letter.[114]

This was Bismarck's last fling before politics took complete and permanent possession of him. When 'Catty' or 'Katsch', as he tenderly called her, met an early death in 1875, Bismarck even lamented the loss in his letter of condolence to Orloff: 'The memory of the time when I experienced this enchantment has accompanied me through the excitements and difficulties of political life as the final reflection of a beautiful day that is no longer.'[115]

On 16 September 1862, Bismarck was back in Paris. Two days later, he received Roon's telegram: 'Danger in delay. Hurry!' The die was cast.

Prime minister in waiting 1862–3

When Bismarck arrived in Berlin on 20 September 1862 after a twenty-five-hour train journey, the conflict over army reform that had been brewing since the spring of 1860 had long since become a full-blown constitutional crisis. The whole thing had seemed quite harmless at first. Not even within the ranks of the liberals was there any dispute as to the necessity of expanding the size of the Prussian army in proportion to the increase of population. But they were suspicious of the government's associated plan to do away with the Landwehr, a product of the Wars of Liberation against Napoleon, while at the same time fixing the period of service at three years. They had good reason to fear that the primary interest of the king and his advisors was not so much to increase military strength as to reinforce the authority of the Crown against the claims of the liberal opposition in the Prussian parliament.

The stiffer the resistance of the liberal majority to approving the funds required for the army reform became, the less inclined Wilhelm I appeared to be to compromise in any way. In March 1862, he dissolved parliament and appointed a new cabinet dominated by the circle of conservative hardliners around the minister for war, Albrecht von Roon. This brought the New Era to a close. The general election of May produced a significant increase in votes for the liberal Progress Party (founded in 1861), while the conservatives were reduced to just a few seats. The lines were more firmly drawn than ever, and by the autumn of 1862, the King seemed to be on the point of abdicating in favour of his son. This was the hour Bismarck had been awaiting for months.

In his decisive conversation with Wilhelm I in Schloss Babelsberg on the afternoon of 22 September, Bismarck understood perfectly how to appeal to the king's feelings by presenting himself as a defender of the rights of the Crown against the repellent parliament: 'I feel like a Brandenburg vassal who sees his overlord in danger.'[116] Not only did Bismarck answer in the affirmative the monarch's question as to whether he was prepared to carry out the reform of the army without restriction, he also bolstered Wilhelm I's view that the conflict with the liberals was essentially a matter of principle – that is, the choice 'between monarchical rule or parliamentary domination; the latter should be resisted at all costs, even by a period of dictatorship'.[117] Bismarck offered himself as the right candidate for this ruthless course of internal struggle, and the king was impressed: 'Then it is my duty to attempt to continue the struggle with you at my side, and I will not abdicate.'

Bismarck's appointment as Prussian prime minister and foreign minister met with overwhelming public rejection, because he was still seen as an ultra-reactionary Junker. The well-known commentator August Ludwig von Rochau, the author of a much-read book, *The Basic Elements of Realpolitik*, wrote: 'With the employment of this man, the sharpest and final bolt of the reaction has been fired ... Though he may have learned and unlearned a few things, he is certainly no fully-fledged statesman, but merely the commonest sort of adventurer who does not look further ahead than the next day.'[118] Those such as Heinrich Abeken, the Legionsrat in the Foreign Office, who knew him better, naturally knew that 'Herr von Bismarck may have had some earlier episodes of youthful excessiveness, but he has become much more sensible and mature, and he should not be expected to act hastily.'[119]

Bismarck's first steps in domestic politics were indeed very cautious, too much so for the liking of his former ultraconservative friends. 'His calm and mildness border on weakness', opined Ludwig von Gerlach.[120] He approached the liberal members of parliament with a mixture of threats and enticements – 'sometimes very rigid ... at others allowing them to sense his desire to reach an accommodation.'[121] For instance, Bismarck's initial concern during the session of the parliamentary budget commission on 30 September 1862 was to ease tensions. As a sign of his readiness to compromise, he took an olive twig out of his cigar case, which Katharina Orloff had given him at their farewell in Avignon. At the same time, he intimated where the potential common ground of the government and the liberals lay: in Prussia adopting a Lesser German policy on the German question – that is, seeking to create a German state that did not include Austria. It was in this context that Bismarck uttered some of his most famous words: 'Germany does not look to Prussia's liberalism, but to its power ... It is not by speeches and motions of a majority that the great questions of the time are decided – that was the great error of 1848 and 1849 – but by iron and blood.'[122] In Bismarck's eyes, these propositions were simply self-evident. His words made an unusually provocative impression on the liberals both within the parliament and outside it, because they seemed to confirm the cliché of Bismarck as a politician of force with no scruples. For Heinrich von Treitschke, these pronouncements on the part of the newcomer were 'the ultimate frivolity': 'When I hear a shallow Junker like this Bismarck boast of "iron and blood", with which he desires to enslave the whole of Germany, it seems to me the baseness of it is exceeded only by the ridiculousness.' Interestingly, Treitschke was later to become one of Bismarck's most ardent admirers.[123]

In view of the storm of public indignation, Bismarck thought it was best to travel out to Jüterbog to meet Wilhelm I on his return at the beginning of October from Baden-Baden, where he had spent a few days, in order to explain his provocative words to the Budget

Commission. In his memoirs, Bismarck recorded with a certain dramatic colour the words with which the king received him in the darkened railway carriage: 'I can see exactly how this will all end. In front of the Opernplatz, beneath my windows, they will strike off your head, and a little later my own.' But if Bismarck's account is to be believed, he managed to raise the king's low spirits by appealing to his sense of honour as a Prussian officer: 'Your Majesty is obliged to fight, you cannot capitulate.'[124]

Now that he had made sure he had the confidence of the king, Bismarck set out on a course of outright confrontation with the liberal opposition. In the middle of October, parliament was adjourned, though an agreement to ratify the army budget was no closer. In practice, since autumn 1862 the prime minister had been governing without the legally prescribed budget. When the Landtag reconvened for a new session at the end of January 1863, Bismarck defended his unconstitutional behaviour by appealing to the so-called gap theory, according to which the constitution was based on an agreement between the three elements of power – crown, parliament and upper house:

> If the agreement is undermined by one of the governing parties attempting to put its own view into effect with doctrinaire absolutism, this series of agreements is interrupted and replaced by conflicts; and because the life of the state cannot stand still, conflicts become questions of power. Whoever has power in his hands will then carry on according to his lights, because the life of the state cannot come to a halt for even an instant.[125]

These words unleashed another storm of protest. To the jubilation of the house, the old liberal Count von Schwerin, who had been Prussia's minister of the interior during the New Era, explained that the prime minister's principle of 'might goes before right' was not a sustainable basis in the long term for the Hohenzollern dynasty. On the contrary, the respect that it enjoyed was based on the principle 'Right goes before might: Justitia fundamentum regnorum! That is the motto of the Prussian kings, and so it will remain'. [126]

Bismarck's position seemed to be untenable, and his fall only a matter of time. 'Our political situation is looking pretty gloomy', wrote Bismarck's banker, Gerson Bleichröder, to Baron James Rothschild. 'The current cabinet is more disliked than almost any other Prussian government before.' [127] In February 1863, the author Theodor Bernhardi observed, 'Everyone regards Bismarck's government as finished and is convinced he can hold out no longer.'[128]

It verges on a miracle that the universally hated and politically isolated 'conflict minister' survived the crisis of spring 1863. To be sure, he employed an arsenal of repressive measures to do so. These were primarily directed against civil servants who adhered to the liberal parliamentary majority or sympathised with it. They were put under pressure to distance themselves from their political endeavours. Anyone who refused could expect to be subject to disciplinary proceedings that often ended in dismissal, the imposition of penalties, or reduced chances of promotion. This illiberal policy towards civil servants was complemented by the gagging of the opposition press. On 1 June 1863, Wilhelm I signed a decree that effectively suspended freedom of the press, 'opening the door to the highest degree of arbitrariness'.[129] The persecution of liberal newspapers and journalists began immediately. There was a flood of warnings and special measures. Many newspaper proprietors bowed to the pressure, fearing financial ruin, and warned their editors to exercise greater restraint. The crown prince, who in any case saw Bismarck's appointment as a serious mistake and disapproved of his confrontational stance in domestic politics, expressly distanced himself from the press decree in a speech of 5 June 1863 in Danzig. 'I declared myself to be an opponent of Bismarck and his pernicious theories, so proving to the world that I did not accept or approve of his system,' he wrote in his diary.[130] But this was no more than a token act, and it made little impression on Bismarck, because he could continue to count on the support of the king.

Just how serious Bismarck felt the situation was is shown by the fact that he toyed with the idea – as a last resort, so to speak – of abolishing the vote and the constitution. 'If there is no other recourse, we might mount a coup,' he had confided to Ludwig von Gerlach as early as November 1862,[131] and during the following months he returned to this idea again and again. In his struggle for political survival, Bismarck was also not afraid of unusual alliances. For instance, in the spring and summer of 1863 he entered into confidential contact with Ferdinand Lassalle, the president of the General German Workers' Association, founded in that year. The common interest of these two very different men was their opposition to the liberals. Bismarck was impressed by his intelligent interlocutor, but he soon broke off relations when he realised that the workers' movement was still too weak to be serviceable to his cause. 'What could Lassalle have offered or given me?' he occasionally asked later. 'He had nothing behind him.'[132]

So the dispute over the army and the constitution lumbered on without coming to a resolution. Bismarck was clearly trying to gain time to gradually wear down the liberal opposition. He kept shocking parliament by making provocative appearances, and subsequently complained that he had been forced 'to listen to unusually tasteless speeches from the mouths of unusually childish and impassioned politicians. These chatterboxes really cannot govern Prussia.'[133] The temptation to break the domestic political stalemate through decisive action in foreign policy was clear.

Yet during his first year in office, Bismarck was denied decisive successes in this arena too. This was true of his first foreign policy undertaking, which the Bismarck hagiographers of earlier decades were inclined to see as the starting point for 'the foundation of Germany as a great power'[134] – the Alvensleben Convention. The background was a rebellion that had broken out in January 1863 in the areas of Poland that were under Russian rule; this threatened to spread to the Polish regions of Prussia. The sympathies of the liberal public throughout Europe were with the rebels, as had been the case in 1830, but Bismarck saw the situation as a welcome opportunity to tighten still further the bond of monarchist solidarity between Prussia and Russia. 'Every success of the Polish nationalist movement is a defeat for Prussia', he had written in November 1861, when he was still the envoy in St Petersburg, 'and we must conduct our fight against these elements according to the rules of war, and not those of civil justice.'[135] The convention that was signed on 8 February 1863 by General Gustav von Alvensleben, who had been sent out to St Petersburg, provided for a correspondingly close collaboration between Russia and Prussia in putting the rebellion down. Amongst other provisions, it permitted the troops of both states to cross the border when in pursuit of rebels who moved between them.

It was not just in the eyes of the liberals that this agreement made Bismarck into the accomplice of the autocratic regime of the tsar; even for a conservative man such as Klemens Theodor Perthes, a jurist and a friend of Albrecht von Roon, it was now clear that Bismarck's appointment 'was a misfortune … and it will bring further misfortune in the future.' The Prussian prime minister now seemed to be 'the very embodiment of unsteadiness and impulsiveness' in the foreign policy of Prussia.[136] The Western powers too, above all Napoleon III, made firm protests against the Prussian intervention, and Bismarck eventually felt obliged to make a diplomatic withdrawal. He gave assurances in Paris and London that the Alvensleben Convention had no practical significance and had not even been formally concluded.

The Vienna government tried to exploit this setback to bring about a reform of the German Confederation corresponding to Austrian interests. On 3 August 1863, Franz Josef invited the Prussian king, who was staying in Bad Gastein to take the waters, to meet him in Frankfurt in mid-August to discuss the plan for reform. In a highly dramatic exchange, Bismarck managed to persuade Wilhelm I to turn down the invitation. The suspicion of the Gerlach circle that the prime minister would not 'confine himself to mere negation and defence' but possibly 'make an entry with a bold counterstroke of his own' was confirmed.[137] In August and September 1863, Bismarck presented the Prussian counterproposals. These demanded parity with Austria, the right of both major German powers to a veto in declarations of war by the German Confederation, and – this was a new element – a 'true National Assembly based on the direct participation of the entire nation'.[138] Bismarck thus made public what he had already hinted at during a private discussion with the liberal politician Viktor von Unruh in July 1859: that Prussia, in furthering its own power interests in Germany, could form an alliance with the liberal nationalist movement.

At a moment when the 'conflict minister' was maintaining the budgetless regime in Prussia and harassing liberal civil servants and newspapers, the renewed demand for a national parliament founded on universal suffrage seemed positively cynical. Bismarck paid for this in the general elections at the end of October 1863, when the liberal opposition gained a clear renewed majority in parliament. But it was during these very weeks that a set of circumstances arose that the liberal commentator Constantin Frantz had clairvoyantly predicted shortly after Bismarck's appointment: 'If Herr von Bismarck succeeds in steering the government [that] he heads towards some bold, lasting, irrevocable act in the German question, within a few days what he said, did or permitted today or yesterday will be forgotten. Then reaction will be at an end, but with it the opposition.'[139]

'I have beaten all of them, every single one!'
1863–7

From the autumn of 1863 onwards, the question of Schleswig-Holstein returned to the centre of German and European politics, and it was this that provided Bismarck with a solution to the bungled domestic political situation. The principalities of Schleswig and Holstein, which were tied to Denmark by a personal union, were a source of strife between German and Danish nationalism. The London Protocol of 1852 had not defused this conflict. In that agreement, the Great Powers had committed themselves to a principle of hereditary succession applying to the Danish monarchy in its entirety, but the special status of the two principalities was also reaffirmed. In March 1863, the Danish king, Friedrich VII, broke the terms of the accord by promulgating a new constitution for the whole state that was aimed at incorporating Schleswig within Denmark. On 13 November, the constitution was ratified by the Danish parliament; two days later, the childless king died. His successor from the Glücksburg line, who ascended the throne in accordance with the London Protocol as Christian IX, was quick to confirm what had been done with his signature.

The German liberal public protested against the incorporation of Schleswig into Denmark. Associations and committees sprang up everywhere, demanding the independence of the principalities. They supported the crown prince, Friedrich von Augustenburg, whom a National Assembly had acclaimed as Friedrich VIII,

Count of Schleswig-Holstein. This too, of course, was a breach of the London Protocol, and conjured up the danger of international complications. For Bismarck, the creation of an independent Schleswig-Holstein under the 'Augustenburger', favoured by the nationalist movement and by a majority of the smaller German states, was always out of the question. His aim was to incorporate the principalities into the Prussian sphere. 'The "United for ever!" will just have to become Prussians', he explained to a small circle of friends around the New Year. 'That is the goal I am heading towards; whether I achieve it is in God's hands.'[140]

He could not, of course, permit his intentions to be known publicly either at home or abroad. The Augustenburger enjoyed some support at the royal court and at the foreign office, as well as among the liberals; Bismarck could certainly not expect any support from the Great Powers for the programme of annexing Schleswig-Holstein. It must without doubt rank as one of his greatest diplomatic achievements that despite all obstacles he attained his goal in the end. Bismarck set to work with unusual skill, carefully planning each step and always leaving alternative options open. At first, he set a highly peaceable tone by appealing to the inviolability of the 1852 agreement. Prussia, he declared, demanded no more of Denmark than strict adherence to the London Protocol. By this strategy he succeeded in deceiving the Great Powers as to his true intentions, and, what was more, he induced Austria to follow the lead of Prussian policy. It was, naturally enough, a matter for relief in Vienna that Bismarck turned a cold shoulder on the nationalist movement and the Augustenburger party, because any 'national' solution would inevitably have set a dangerous precedent for the multinational Habsburg state.

This temporary solidarity between the two major German powers also meant that the Bundestag in Frankfurt could largely be prevented from influencing the course of events. Bismarck explained his intentions in his Christmas letter of 1863 to the Prussian envoy in Paris, Robert von der Golz, who did not understand this shift in Prussian diplomacy:

> If we now turn our back on the Great Powers and throw ourselves into the arms of the policy of the small states, a policy which is entangled in the network of democratic associations, the resulting situation for the monarchy at home and abroad would be the most wretched imaginable ... Growth in our power cannot derive from cabinet and press politics; it must come from armed Great Power politics, and we do not have sufficient sustained strength to squander it in the wrong cause, for slogans and for Augustenburg.[141]

Equipped with a mandate for federal action, on 16 January Prussia and Austria delivered an ultimatum to the Danish government, demanding that it return to the determinations of the London Protocol and threatening to occupy Schleswig if Denmark did not comply. After the ultimatum was rejected, Prussian and Austrian troops under the overall command of the Prussian field marshal Friedrich von Wrangel began to march into Schleswig. From the beginning, Bismarck intended to extend the war from Schleswig to neighbouring Jutland, into which the bulk of the Danish forces had withdrawn. If the army achieved a spectacular success on the battlefield, Bismarck was counting on this bringing it greater prestige, which could be used as political capital in the domestic struggle against the liberal opposition. Prussia was still hoping for 'some military deeds of renown', as Bleichröder, the banker, reported to Paris at the end of February 1864: 'It seems these are essential for the glory of the army.'[142] When the Dybbol redoubts were stormed on 18 April 1864, the Prussian troops indeed achieved a great victory, though at the cost of heavy losses.

The storming of the Dybbol redoubts by Prussian troops on 18 April 1864.

Just as Bismarck expected, news of the victory was received with wide public enthusiasm. 'The Prussians have given a new shine to their ancient military fame, Napoleon has been taught a lesson, the organisation of the army is saved, the nation rejoices, and Bismarck is ever more popular', enthused Wilhelm von Kügelgen, a lord-in-waiting at the court of Anhalt-Bernburg, just after receiving the news.[143] The example of Heinrich von Treitschke shows that not even the liberals remained unimpressed: 'The way the brave troops stormed in', he wrote in May 1864, 'betrays once more that vein of greatness that has never been entirely lacking in this state ... At long last, something true and worthy amongst all this mouthing of slogans! I was as pleased as Punch.'[144]

Just two days after the storming of the Dybbol redoubts, an international conference was convened in London at the request of England. Now that the London Protocol of 1852 had served its purpose in Bismarck's eyes, he did everything he could to complicate negotiations to such an extent that a solution acceptable to all sides receded into the far distance. On 25 June, the participants in the conference went their separate ways without a result; a few days later, Prussia and Austria resumed the war, and in the preliminary peace agreement of Vienna of 1 August 1864 and the definitive Treaty of Vienna of 30 October, they compelled Denmark to cede all rights in the two principalities to the Prussian king and the Austrian emperor.

With this, Bismarck had achieved his initial goal of separating Schleswig-Holstein from Denmark. Now he could set his sights on the second stage, the annexation of the principalities by Prussia. Austria would never willingly consent to this, and so Bismarck's primary concern was how to go about compelling Vienna to recognise such a decisive extension of Prussian power within Germany. This inevitably raised the larger question of Prusso-Austrian dualism, which Bismarck, in his days as ambassador in Frankfurt, had seen as absolutely necessary to resolve in the long term. To this end, he was able to turn the joint Prusso-Austrian administration of the principalities agreed in the Treaty of Vienna to advantage because he could at any time exploit the frictions that inevitably arose in the course of the partnership in order to escalate conflict with Austria. Yet it would be incorrect to assume that he single-mindedly pursued a course leading to war from autumn 1864 onwards. Such an early and definite decision went against the guiding principle of his diplomacy, the success of which lay in its attempt to keep alternative options open as long as this was at all possible. This meant that a peaceful resolution was in no way excluded in advance, though from spring 1865 onwards the likelihood of this increasingly receded.

In mid-August 1865, it seemed that Prussia and Austria would reach a negotiated settlement after all. In the Gastein Convention, they agreed to divide the principalities: Schleswig would be ruled by the Austrians and Holstein by the Prussians. In internal diplomatic correspondence, Bismarck more than once made clear that the agreement that had been achieved had only 'put off the decisive settling of accounts with Austria'.[145] At the same time, he also described it as 'desirable not to allow the break to become an immediate necessity too soon'.[146] For Bismarck, the main thing was now to find the most propitious moment for the conflict. Since autumn 1865 at the latest, it had been clear to him that the decision as to the future of the principalities was also inextricably linked to resolving the question of a German nation state. Just a few weeks after the Gastein Convention, he dictated to his executive secretary Robert von Keudell, 'The question of Schleswig-Holstein is so closely linked to the great German question that, if it comes to an open rift, we must resolve both together.'[147]

At a session of the Privy Council on 28 February, the course was set for war, but without any definite decision being made. Bismarck, who in the previous few weeks had crossed swords anew with the liberal opposition, asserted quite baldly 'that domestic circumstances do not make a foreign war necessary, but they may be an additional reason for making it seem advantageous'.[148] In other words, the Prussian prime minister expected a war not only to decide who was to be master of Germany, but also to bring about a solution to the constitutional crisis that had now been dragging on for more than three years. Wilhelm I still had an instinctive horror at the thought of a 'fraternal war', and Bismarck continually had to deploy all his powers of persuasion to prevent the king changing his mind. According to those in the know in Berlin, the prime minister had to 'wind the king up again' like a watchmaker tending to a clock.[149]

The months following the Privy Council were a time of great tension for Bismarck. 'Our friend Otto B., his nerves worn out by Herculean labours day and night, now has to contend with the rebellion of his truest and most loyal subject till now, his stomach', wrote Roon in concern in March 1866 to Moritz von Blankenburg.[150] Bismarck sought all means to isolate Austria diplomatically, and at the same time to provoke it, while still keeping a back door open in case changes in the general political situation interfered with his plans. He could be to some degree confident of Russia's neutrality; the country was occupied with internal political problems, and in any case it too had had a hostile attitude to Austria since the time of the Crimean War. The relationship with France was trickier. With great finesse, Bismarck managed to ensure the neutrality of Napoleon III by raising the prospect of compensations – though without entering into any binding agreement. The final element of the diplomatic preparations for war against Austria was a secret treaty with Italy signed on 8 April 1866. In it, Italy undertook to enter the war on Prussia's side in exchange for the prospective acquisition of Venetia. The treaty was limited to a period of three months, however, so that the decision had to be taken one way or the other before it expired.

Bismarck lit the fuse just one day later, when he instructed the Prussian ambassador in Frankfurt, Karl Friedrich von Savigny, to propose the creation of a German parliament based on general direct suffrage. This was the second time Bismarck had played the nationalist democratic card, and was bound to be deeply irritating to Austria because it put the very existence of the multinational Hapsburg state into question. In Viennese diplomatic circles, many were also outraged at Bismarck's use of the word 'parliament', which, coming from him, 'appeared to be just a frivolous slogan'.[151] The Prussian conservatives were indignant too. 'What do you make of this latest twist of Bismarck's?' wrote Adolph von Kleist to Ludwig von Gerlach on 10 April. 'Appealing to national sovereignty!!! The formation of a Constituent Assembly!! ... Our allies: nothing but revolutionaries of all stripes ... This leaves us in a daze.' [152] In an article in the *Kreuzzeitung* on 8 May 1866, Gerlach took a firm stand against resolving the problem of Prusso-Austrian dualism through war, and he condemned the proposed reform of the Confederation as a 'fundamentally revolutionary project ... that deeply wounds the heart of Germany and at the same time the heart of Prussia and Austria.' [153] The article was seen on all sides as a sensation, for Gerlach was thus distancing himself publicly for the first time from his former political protégé.

It was not just among Prussian conservatives that the 'fraternal war' taking shape was unpopular. 'The whole country was clearly against the war', as Rudolf von Delbrück recollected. [154] Economic life was stifled by the fear of a long, injurious conflict; at the beginning of May 1866, the bottom seemed to drop out of the stock market. On the afternoon of 7 May, the twenty-two-year-old Württemberg student Ferdinand Cohn-Blind – a stepson of Karl Blind, who had been a revolutionary in Baden in 1848–9 and now lived in exile in London – fired several shots at the Prussian prime minister on Unter den Linden. As though by a miracle, Bismarck was uninjured, and he took this as a good omen. Particularly in the southern German states, Bismarck's assailant – who took his own life in prison – met with some public sympathy. The Bonn historian Heinrich von Sybel, who was later to become a Bismarck hagiographer, wrote a week after the attack, 'Everything is dominated by the bitter, persistent general hatred that internal misrule has generated over the past four years; unfortunately Bismarck himself is the personal focus of it, because of his importance and his idiosyncratic manner.' [155]

From the beginning of June 1866, things rapidly came to a head. On 1 June, the Vienna government submitted the decision as to the future of Schleswig-Holstein to the Bundestag in Frankfurt, without first consulting Prussia. Bismarck answered this breach of the Gastein Convention by sending Prussian troops into Holstein. On 14 June, the Bundestag decided, at the request of Austria, to mobilise the Confederation's army against Prussia. In response, the Prussian ambassador to the Confederation declared the federal treaty to be void. On 16 June, after an ultimatum had been rejected, Prussian troops moved against Hanover, Saxony and the Electorate of Hesse. This marked the commencement of hostilities. Bismarck must have realised that he was gambling everything on a single throw of the dice. On the evening of 15 June, he said to the British ambassador, Lord Loftus, 'It may be that Prussia will lose, but whatever the outcome, the country will fight with bravery and honour. If we are beaten ... I will not return to Berlin. I will fall at the final attack.'[156]

This pronouncement was not put to the test, for the Prussian troops won a decisive victory at the Battle of Königgrätz (or Sadowa) on 3 July 1866. On this epochal event, *The Spectator* commented: 'Overnight Prussia has seized a place as the leading Great Power of Europe.'[157] The fortunate outcome of the battle filled Bismarck with satisfaction: 'I have beaten all of them, every single one!'[158] Yet even at the hour of his greatest triumph he kept a cool head – quite unlike Wilhelm I and many of his soldiers, who would have preferred to take Vienna and impose harsh conditions on their humiliated opponent. But in light of the situation of Europe as a whole, for Bismarck moderation in victory above all was a commandment of diplomatic foresight. He wrote to his wife on 9 July:

> If we do not exaggerate our demands, if we do not believe we have conquered the world, then we will achieve a peace that is worth having. But we become intoxicated as quickly as we lose heart, and I have the thankless task of pouring cold water into the seething wine, and making the point that we do not dwell alone in Europe; but with three other powers that hate and envy us.[159]

Considerable further struggle was needed to convince the monarch that Prussia must 'regard the Austrian state as a useful piece on the European chessboard, and the renewal of good relations with it as a possible move we should keep open for ourselves'.[160] In the preliminary Peace of Nikolsburg on 26 July, Bismarck was able to impose his ideas in all essentials, and this was confirmed in the definitive Treaty of Prague on 23 August. Austria did not have to cede any territory, but it had to agree to the dissolution of the German Confederation and the reorganisation under Prussian leadership of Germany to the north of the Main river. Schleswig-Holstein was annexed, together with Hanover, the Electorate of Hesse, Nassau and the free city of Frankfurt. When it came to the filling-out of Prussian power in northern Germany, Bismarck was anything but self-restrained, and Saxony too almost fell victim to his desire for annexation. The link between the eastern and western regions of Prussia, an important goal of Prussian policy ever since the Congress of Vienna in 1815, was thus created; the territorial integrity of the southern states, Baden, Württemburg and Bavaria, was guaranteed, but without excluding the possibility of closer links in future between the planned North German Confederacy and a Southern Confederacy, as yet unfounded. Further unification to form a national state was thus not blocked, but it seemed it was to be put on hold for the time being.

Bismarck's intention was to follow up the conclusion of peace abroad with a resolution of the domestic situation, that is, to take advantage of this favourable moment to finally bring to an end the conflict with the opposition in the Prussian parliament. Between June and July 1866, the country's mood had clearly shifted in favour of the once-hated 'conflict minister', so the liberals too were now more open to compromise. The change was reflected in the elections of 3 July, which had brought the conservatives an increase of more than 100 seats – before the news of the Battle of Königgrätz arrived.

The unexpectedly quick and decisive victory made even the most strongly principled among the liberals waver in their judgement of Bismarck. Theodor Mommsen, the ancient historian, suddenly felt 'a marvellous sensation of being there when history is turning a corner.'[161] The Göttingen jurist Rudolf von Ihering, who only in May had condemned the looming war as 'a gruesome frivolity', now made obeisance 'before the genius of Bismarck, who has pulled off a brilliant stroke of political manoeuvring seldom exampled in history'.[162]

The bridge of gold Bismarck built to the liberals was the announcement in a speech by Wilhelm I at the opening of parliament on 5 August 1866 that the government would ask parliament for 'indemnity', that is, retrospective approval of its expenditure. This implied the recognition that since 1862 the government had in practice been carried on without a legal basis. This announcement had an explosive effect within the liberal camp in parliament. Why, argued more and more of their spokesmen, should they stubbornly persist in opposition when the Prussian prime minister was now himself offering the hand of compromise, and when progress in the German question could be expected so soon as a result of his decisive policy? Those who warned against the cult of success, and reminded the others that the recognition of liberal freedoms must have priority over bringing about national unity, were increasingly marginalised. On 3 September 1866, the Indemnity Bill was passed by 230 votes to 75; the majority of the liberal opposition too voted in favour. This brought the constitutional conflict to an end, and with it the unity of the Progress Party. In the course of the following months the moderates, who unequivocally favoured cooperation with the Prussian prime minister, joined ranks to form the National Liberal Party. In November 1866, one of the new party's spokesmen, Karl Twesten, formulated its credo: 'The liberals must not question the power of the state again!'[163] Nor did the conservatives survive the break of 1866 without division. A group of moderate supporters of realpolitik broke off from the old conservatives, who remained true to their original principles, to form the Free Conservative Party in 1867. It supported Bismarck's policy without reservation.

It was not just the old Prussian conservatives who felt that the sudden changes of 1866, which overthrew the established balance of power in Germany and sent the party system into tumult, were practically revolutionary. For example, in June 1866 the constitutional lawyer Johann Caspar Bluntschli spoke of a 'German revolution in the form of a war, led from above rather than below, in accordance with the nature of monarchy'.[164] At the end of the year, Heinrich von Treitschke opined, 'Our revolution is being completed from above, just as it was begun, and we, with the limited understanding of subordinates, remain in the dark.' [165] The concept of the 'revolution from above' was used to describe the vexing fact that this upheaval, felt to be revolutionary, had been set in motion by the Prussian government itself, and was quite clearly meant to serve the interests of conservative and Greater Prussian domination. In July 1866, Bismarck summarised this seeming paradox with a characteristic turn of phrase: 'If there is to be revolution, then we would rather make it ourselves than be its victims.'[166] That he meant this seriously was proved by the ruthlessness with which he sacrificed the principle of dynastic legitimacy in Hanover, Kurhessen and Nassau to the expansion of Prussian power, and also by his demand for a parliament to be convened on the basis of equal and general suffrage. This 'unambiguous, genuine commitment to the basic revolutionary principle, made before the eyes of all Europe', as Klemens Theodor Perthes described the federal reform proposal of 9 April 1866,[167] was no idle threat. On the contrary, it was put into effect in the 1867 constitution of the North German Federation.

This constitution was entirely the work of Bismarck. He wrote an outline of its features during October and November in Putbus on the island of Rügen, where he had gone to renew his strength, which was exhausted by the exceptional tensions of the prior months. Here, in the seclusion of the Baltic island, tended to by his wife, he found the leisure he needed to think through all aspects of the innovation. His principal objection to the various preliminary drafts of his collaborators was that their tendency was 'too much that of a centralised federal state for the southern German states to join in the future. The form', he explained in his famous 'Putbus diktat', 'will have to be closer to a confederacy of states; but in practice, it must be given the nature of a federal state by the use of elastic and seemingly harmless, but far-reaching expressions'.[168]

Bismarck's aim was precisely to achieve a flexible adjustment of the existing forms and institutions to the new political forces and situation. The basic idea from which everything else derived was, of course, to cement Prussian domination as effectively and lastingly as possible. For example, the head of the federation of states was called the Bundespräsidium, along the lines of the familiar terminology of the German Confederation, but this office was filled by none other than the wearer of the Prussian crown, who was equipped with extensive powers, including the overall command of the Federal Army, the power to declare war and peace, and the right to appoint and dismiss the federal chancellor. In the Federal Council that was based on the old Frankfurt parliament, seventeen of forty-three delegates were to be supplied by Prussia, the largest member state. This meant the Prussian veto would always be able to prevent any change in the constitution, for which a two-thirds majority was required. The Federal Council was presided over by the federal chancellor, who was at the same time Prussian prime minister and foreign minister.

There can hardly be any doubt that Bismarck intended from the outset to assume the chancellorship himself; the unusual accumulation of offices opened up possibilities that went far beyond those available to the Prussian envoy. In this respect, the constitution of the North German Federation had in view not only the Prussian claim to hegemony, but also Bismarck's personal ambition for power. The unitary counterbalance to the Federal Council, representing individual states, was to be the Reichstag, or Imperial Parliament, representing the people. Bismarck conceded universal suffrage in the hope of strengthening the conservative, royalist electorate and weakening the liberals. 'In a country with a monarchist tradition and a loyal disposition, universal suffrage will lead to monarchist elections by undermining the influence of the liberal middle class', he had pronounced as early as April 1866.[169]

The election of the preliminary Reichstag on 12 February 1867 did not fully confirm this expectation. The new National Liberal Party emerged as the strongest party, with seventy-nine seats, followed by the Conservatives (fifty-nine) and the Free Conservatives (thirty-nine). The Progress Party only achieved nineteen seats, making it the real loser. In the discussions on the draft constitution, the National Liberal Party managed to negotiate some concessions from Bismarck, such as complementing universal direct suffrage with the secret ballot. But he remained immovable on two points: the military budget was largely removed from parliamentary control, and there were no federal ministries responsible to parliament, meaning that the Reichstag could bring down neither the chancellor nor the members of his government. Bismarck had made considerable concessions to the demands of the middle class and the liberals in the form of democratic elections and a parliamentary legislature, but at the same time he had taken strong measures against any attempt to further develop the constitutional system under the primacy of the Prussian monarchy into a parliamentary system. In the end, the constitution of the North German Federation, which was passed with a large majority on 16 August 1867, was also a triumph for Bismarck, who got his way on all decisive points.

The Founder of the Reich 1866–71

The successes that Bismarck had achieved since 1864 were recognised in numerous ways. In 1865, Wilhelm I made him a count. In 1866, after the victory over Austria and once the indemnity had been granted, the Prussian parliament rewarded him with an endowment of 400,000 talers; this made Bismarck a rich man overnight. He used a large part of the money to buy the estate of Varzin in Upper Pomerania – an enormous area of over 22,500 acres, half of which was forest, which Bismarck loved. 'There, I have more to say to the trees than to people,' he once admitted to his wife.[170] He was still not satisfied with what he had acquired, and was continually dreaming up ways to extend his territory by adding the neighbouring estates to it. 'Every evening [he] experienced a tremendous appetite for annexing these lands', as he told his old student friend Count Alexander Keyserling in October 1868, 'but in the morning [he] could gaze at them calmly'.[171]

In politics too, Bismarck did not pause after 1866. Amongst close friends he made it quite clear that as far as he was concerned the River Main did not constitute a final border; it was just a staging post on the road to German unity. If his central aim up to 1866 had been to strengthen Prussia's position, now his policy was dominated by the project of creating a Lesser German nation state under Prussian leadership.[172] This does not mean that Bismarck was suddenly moved by previously repressed national feeling, being turned into a German 'patriot' rather than a Prussian one. If he allied himself with the idea of the nation and the movement that promoted it, that was because he believed this was the only way to mobilise the social leverage he needed to pursue the unification of the North German Federation with the southern states, as he sought to do. He certainly saw this as quite a long-term goal: 'If Germany achieves its national aim in the nineteenth century, that seems to me a great thing, and if it were to be in ten or even five years, that would be something extraordinary, an unhoped-for gift by the grace of God', he said in 1868.[173]

First and foremost, Bismarck had to allow for the opposition of France. Napoleon III, together with large sections of the French public, was deeply perturbed by the Prussian victory of 1866, which had so clearly altered the balance of European power to the disadvantage of France. Under the slogan 'Revenge for Sadowa' (that is, Königgrätz), the French demanded compensation in the form of territorial acquisitions. Their gaze turned to the Grand Duchy of Luxembourg, which had belonged to the German Confederation and sheltered a federal fortress with a Prussian garrison. At first, Bismarck allowed the French government to think he had no objection in principle to ceding the territory, but he indicated they should enter into direct negotiations with King William III of the Netherlands, to whom the Grand Duchy was tied in a personal union. But simultaneously he did all he could to undermine the French plans. As a warning, on 19 March 1867 he published the secret mutual assistance treaties that Prussia had concluded with the southern German states. Through the press and the platform of the North German Reichstag, he provoked the French mood. The Luxembourg Crisis was eventually resolved at an international conference in London at the end of May 1867. The Grand Duchy received neutral status, and Prussia had to agree to remove its garrison. Paris felt tricked because it had been denied a prestigious success. From then on, Napoleon III was determined to block any further expansion of Prussian power.

Bismarck also met with unexpectedly vigorous resistance from the southern German states. His hope that the North German Federation would operate as a magnet here was not realised. However, the extensive legislative work completed by the North German Reichstag after 1867, in close cooperation with the bureaucrats of the Prussian ministries, particularly Rudolf von Delbrück, head of the Federal Chancellor's office, was an impressive achievement. It included, for instance, a law granting freedom of movement, a comprehensive set of trade regulations, the introduction of unified weights and measures, and a criminal code. 'It was a brilliant period of reform that laid the foundations of business life and modern civil society; these have lasted up to the present day', as the historian Hans-Ulrich Wehler characterised this astonishingly successful record.[174]

The dominant feeling among the southern German governments, however, was fear of being 'Prussified' by the great north German power. Bismarck's endeavours to draw the south gradually closer to the North German Federation by means of cooperation over military and economic policy were received with considerable reserve. In July 1867, a delegation of the member states of the Customs Union decided to convene a Customs Parliament, voting for which was to be according to the Reichstag electoral rules, but the results of the first elections were a bitter disappointment for Bismarck. In Bavaria and Württemberg, the opponents of closer links with the North German Federation gained clear majorities, and the adherents of a Lesser German policy unexpectedly found themselves on the defensive. This put an end to hopes of using the Customs Parliament as the 'germ and core of the unification process'.[175] Bismarck's conclusion was that he would have to be patient for the time being regarding the realisation of the national goal. In a memorandum of 26 February 1869 to the Prussian ambassador in Munich, Georg Freiherr von Werthern, he warned against 'the wordy agitation with which people outside government circles seek for a philosopher's stone that could bring about German unity immediately', arguing that 'an arbitrary interference in the development of history that is based on merely subjective reasons has only ever led to the bringing down of unripe fruit, and in my opinion it is obvious that German unity is not a ripe fruit at this moment'.[176]

In Bismarck's view, what was needed to overcome the stagnation in the German question was an external threat, coming if at all possible from France, which would enable him to trump the virulence of anti-Prussian feeling in southern Germany with an appeal to German nationalist sentiment. Bismarck waited for such a situation, in which Prussia would be able to act defensively against some supposed aggression.

The dispute about the candidacy for the Spanish throne in 1869 and 1870 seemed to present a perfect and unexpected opportunity. In September 1868, Spanish soldiers led by General Prim had toppled Queen Isabella II. In the search for a suitable candidate for the vacant throne, Prince Leopold, the crown prince of the house of Hohenzollern-Sigmaringen, who was married to a Portuguese princess, came into consideration. From the beginning, Bismarck had followed developments in the question of the Spanish succession attentively. 'It lies in our interest', he instructed the foreign office on 3 October 1868, 'to leave the Spanish question open as a possibility of peace, and a solution to Napoleon's liking can hardly be one that will be useful to us'.[177] Not much imagination was required to see that the candidacy of a Hohenzollern prince to the Spanish throne would inevitably meet with strong resistance from France. Bismarck immediately recognised the opportunity this might present to provoke a military conflict, though this does not mean that he had taken a very long view – from as early as 1868 – in planning the war with France, working deliberately towards it. He first paid close attention to the whole situation in spring 1870, after an emissary of the Spanish government formally submitted the offer of the candidacy. Bismarck was now determined to force the issue and to take full advantage of its potential for conflict.

There has been much dispute in historical research about Bismarck's motives and intentions.[178] An important role was clearly played by the expectation that an intensification of Franco-Prussian antagonisms could lead Lesser German nationalism out of the dead end in which it had found itself since 1868. But this meant manoeuvring France into a situation where it would appear to be the aggressor, and Prussia the victim. Only if this were achieved could Bismarck hope to carry the southern German states along with the plan and transform the skirmish with France into a national war that could achieve German unity. He could also only count on keeping the other powers out of the conflict if he managed to present Prussia as the victim of apparent French aggression.

There can be no doubt about Bismarck's willingness to pursue a course of conflict with France. In spring 1870, he described 'a rapid war with France' as an 'inevitable necessity' to Saxony's minister of state, Richard von Friesen.[179] However, this did not mean that he wanted to bring this war about under any circumstances. As usual, he still kept alternatives open in case things did not develop according to his plans. There were certainly plenty of uncertain factors. Wilhelm I and even Karl Anton von Hohenzollern-Sigmaringen, the father of the candidate for the throne, had strong doubts about his candidature. Numerous tactical manoeuvres and secret diplomatic missions to Madrid were needed before Crown Prince Leopold officially accepted the Spanish offer on 19 June, and the Prussian king gave his agreement two days later. To give the impression he had nothing to do with any of it, Bismarck retired to his estate at Varzin during the critical weeks.

On 2 July, the 'Spanish bomb' exploded when the press published the news of the candidature before the planned announcement.

No-one in Paris was taken in by Bismarck's fiction that the whole thing was a purely dynastic matter that the Prussian government itself had no hand in. In a sensational speech before the chamber on 6 July, the French foreign minister, the Duc de Gramont, threatened that France would not allow the Hohenzollerns to put one of their princes on the throne of Charles V, so prejudicing the balance of power in Europe as well as the 'honour of France'. Bismarck's reaction when he read the text of the speech on 8 July in Varzin – seemingly astonished, but in reality delighted at the news – was to say, 'It certainly looks like war.'[180] From this moment on, his only concern was to unleash the war under the most favourable conditions possible. The French government made this easier for him by not accepting Prince Karl Anton's official withdrawal on 12 July of his son's candidature to the throne; they demanded that Wilhelm I, as head of the House of Hohenzollern, should renounce the claim permanently, as well as declaring that he had not meant to injure France's honour or interests. This naturally went too far. Wilhelm I politely but firmly rejected this humiliating request, which was brought to him in the town of Bad Ems by Benedetti, the French ambassador. Bismarck used the telegram in which the king informed him of what had happened there to bring about the very combination of circumstances he had had in mind from the start. By provocatively sharpening the tone of this so-called Ems Dispatch and immediately making the text public, he left Napoleon III little choice but to respond with a declaration of war on 19 July.

Bismarck's strategy of a 'disguised provocation to war'[181] had come off: France seemed to the whole world to be the troublemaker, whereas Bismarck, who was the true aggressor, was able to play the role of the persecuted innocent. German public opinion almost universally took the side of Prussia, supposedly the threatened party. This meant the mutual assistance treaties with the southern German states were triggered. France, on the other hand, found itself

Napoleon III and Bismarck after the French Emperor's surrender at Sedan on 2 September 1870.

completely isolated. No European power seemed inclined to come to its aid. To ensure the neutrality of Great Britain, Bismarck took an unusual step that went against the customs of secret diplomacy by leaking to the *Times* in London a handwritten draft treaty drawn up by Benedetti in 1866; this was meant to show that Napoleon had intended at the time to annexe Belgium and Luxembourg by force.

As in the war against Austria, the strategy of Helmuth von Moltke, Prussian chief of staff, was to seek a rapid decision. After a series of successful opening battles, in mid-August the main force of the French army was enclosed in the fortress of Metz. At the beginning of September, an army that came to relieve them under MacMahon was cut off at Sedan and routed. Napoleon III became a prisoner of war, and the Bonapartist regime collapsed. Unlike in 1866, however, this did not bring the war to an end. On 4 September, a 'government of national defence' was proclaimed, and it organised the resistance. The 'cabinet war' expanded to become a national war. All attempts to break through the besieging forces that had surrounded Paris since the end of September failed, but in the occupied areas French guerrillas, the so-called 'francs-tireurs', did considerable small-scale damage to German forces.

Bismarck, who was accompanying the German advance with a small staff from the Foreign Office, was furious at the unexpectedly stubborn resistance of the French. He demanded the most severe reprisals against the francs-tireurs. 'Our people are splendid at shooting, but not when it comes to executions', he complained. 'All villages where there is a betrayal should immediately be burned down, and all the male inhabitants should be hanged.'[182] This was not just an isolated aberration; such statements are recorded again and again in different forms in the diary of his press spokesman Moritz Busch, reflecting a horrifying brutality of thought that conveys a foretaste of future German crimes in the two world wars. This hatred for the francs-tireurs was combined with a profound dislike of the French as a people. Bismarck's choice remarks at table on the supposed character of the French were on the level of a bar-room bigot: 'France is a nation of zeroes, a herd; they have money and elegance, but no individuals ... thirty million clots, none of them with any character or worth – they cannot even be compared to the Italians and Russians, let alone to us Germans.'[183] The fact that this nation he detested was defending itself so bravely against the invasion was especially annoying to Bismarck.

The chancellor of the North German Federation wore uniform throughout the campaign – one more reason for the general staff to make fun of the 'civilian in a cuirassier's uniform',[184] who was in their opinion constantly meddling in their business. Bismarck for his part made no bones about his reservations when it came to the army leadership; he complained that they did not let him in on their plans sufficiently. During the course of the war, these mutual animosities increased, and in the dispute that ran for several months as to the utility of bombarding Paris, they grew into a conflict of principle between the political and military command. Bismarck wanted the capital to be softened up for an assault so as to shorten the war; he was frightened that the other Great Powers might intervene. Moltke, on the other hand, was hoping to starve the city out. One senior member of the general staff said that as far as he was concerned its inhabitants should 'snuff it like rabid dogs'.[185] In the end, Bismarck got his way. From December 1870 onwards, the outlying forts surrounding Paris were under constant bombardment from the German artillery.

It was not so much the military policy of the General Staff that contributed to lengthening the war as the demand to annexe Alsace and parts of Lorraine. This had first been suggested here and there at the end of June 1870, and after the first German victories in August 1870 a flood of articles and pamphlets declared it to be the most important German war aim. This movement in favour of annexation was not inspired by Bismarck, as has sometimes been maintained.[186] However, after mid-August the chancellor had become convinced, quite independently of public opinion, that it was essential to separate Alsace-Lorraine from France, because the lasting hostility of France was to be expected in the future. 'Our victory at Sadowa aroused bitterness in the French; how much the more will our victory over France itself do so!' he wrote on 21 August. 'The only correct policy under such circumstances, if we have an enemy of whom we cannot make a solid friend, is to make him at least somewhat less dangerous, and to protect ourselves more against him.'[187] Control of the strategically important deployment zone in Alsace seemed to be the minimum to be demanded in the interests of German security. Without doubt, the decision to annexe the territory was a serious error, perhaps the most serious in all of Bismarck's career, because as well as provoking far more strenuous resistance on the part of the French population it cemented the enmity between Germany and France long after the war itself ended.

Bismarck wanted to induce the southern German states to join the North German Federation before the campaign was over, without direct compulsion and on the basis of freely negotiated treaties. As he had expected, the patriotic enthusiasm that greeted the beginning of the war had spread to southern Germany too, where it put the opponents of unification on the defensive. From mid-October, he held negotiations in Versailles with delegations from each southern German state; these were conducted with each country separately. Their first success came on 15 November, when Baden and Hesse-Darmstadt joined the North German Federation. A few 'reserved rights' had to be conceded to Bavaria and Württemburg, particularly in military matters, but only a few days later they too resolved to take this step. After the treaty with Bavaria was signed on 23 November, Bismarck proclaimed, 'German unity has been created, and the Kaiser too'.[188]

But this did not mean that there were no further obstacles. Wilhelm I resisted the title 'German Kaiser', and his dislike of it would probably have been still more pronounced had he known that the letter in which King Ludwig II of Bavaria offered him the title had not only been drafted by Bismarck, but had been purchased with bribes from the Welfenfonds, or Guelph Fund, a secret fund derived from the former property of the House of Hanover. For Bismarck, it was politically essential to appeal to the symbolism of the old Reich, because he hoped this would help to integrate the non-Prussian population into the new Lesser German state. These disagreements about the title continued until just before the Proclamation of the German Empire in the Hall of Mirrors at Versailles that had been arranged for 18 January 1871. The famous painting by the court artist Anton von Werner gives the impression of an atmosphere of celebration, but if anything it was subdued. Shortly

The Imperial Proclamation in the Hall of Mirrors in Versailles on 18 January 1871, by Anton von Werner.

afterwards, Bismarck, who was 'in a terrible mood and unusually irritable',[189] wrote to his wife:

> The birth of the Kaiser was not an easy one. At such times kings have whimsical urges, just like women before they bring that into the world which they cannot any longer contain within themselves. As midwife there were several moments when I felt a pressing need to be a bomb and explode, reducing the whole edifice to smithereens.[190]

A few days after the proclamation, Paris capitulated. Tough negotiations with Jules Favre, the representative of the French provisional government, led to the signing of a ceasefire on 28 January 1871, followed exactly a month later by the preliminary peace and, in Frankfurt on 10 May, by the definitive peace treaty. Bismarck was at the peak of his political career. He was made a prince, and Wilhelm I gifted him the Saxon Forest just outside Hamburg. The chancellor was heaped with medals and honours, but even now he remained free of triumphalism. He was only too aware of the precariousness of the new national state that had been founded on three wars. 'People just have no idea of the true situation,' he said in conversation at table in Versailles in early December 1870. 'We are balancing on the top of a lightning conductor; if we lose the balance I have made such an effort to bring about, we will fall to the ground.'[191] From then on, all Bismarck's thoughts and plans were aimed at preserving what had been achieved.

Consolidation and preservation 1871–85

The creation of the Lesser German and Greater Prussian German national state led to unease throughout Europe, even where the process of unification had at first been followed with sympathetic but distant interest, as in England. The formation of a new and powerful state in the middle of the continent shook the traditional European balance to the core. Worse still, the new German Reich that had been baptised at Versailles seemed to be about to try and take on a hegemonic role. Bismarck was conscious that he could only allay such fears by strictly limiting the aims of German foreign policy and renouncing all further territorial claims. He could only hope that other states would gradually become reconciled to the existence of the Reich if he declared it to be 'saturated'; in February 1874, he made a typical assurance: 'Our policy is one of security and not of power.'[192] To be sure, after 1871 the founder of the Reich did not turn overnight into a consistently peaceful leader, as the Bismarck orthodoxy long asserted. Rather, his diplomacy in the early 1870s was characterised by a degree of uncertainty as to the best ways and means. Bismarck needed to go through a learning process to adapt to the unaccustomed role of self-moderation.

He of course strove incessantly to weaken and isolate republican France to such an extent that it could never pose a threat to Germany; after the annexation of Alsace-Lorraine, the permanent enmity of the French was to be expected. To this end, Bismarck sought to strengthen the traditionally friendly links with Russia while at the same time normalising relations with Austria. It became one of the basic principles of his foreign policy to retain good relations with both powers without having to opt for one or the other. In the so-called League of Three Emperors in October 1873, the three countries agreed to act jointly to preserve peace in Europe. However, the fragility of this agreement soon showed itself in the War in Sight crisis of spring 1875, which Bismarck himself provoked, highly alarmed as he was by developments in foreign policy since 1874. France had recovered from the war with unexpected rapidity, and was preparing to make itself once more a force to be reckoned with among the Great Powers. At the same time, there were disquieting indications that Russian diplomacy was putting out feelers to the Quai d'Orsay. For the first time, the chancellor of the Reich was confronted with the nightmare possibility of a Franco-Russian coalition, a nightmare that was not to leave him for the rest of his time in office. To be sure, Bismarck did not intend to let loose another war. At the beginning of April 1875, he unfolded a press campaign intended to put France firmly in its place; at the same time, he wanted to test the reactions of the other powers to see how much political room for manoeuvre was available to Germany.

This time, however, Bismarck had overplayed his hand. Britain and Russia temporarily closed ranks against his threatening policy and took concerted action. Their joint intervention in Berlin in May 1875 made it clear that they would not tolerate any further alteration in the balance of power in Central Europe to the advantage of Germany. This was a major blow for Bismarck. He was clearly presented with the limits he could not overstep if he did not want to threaten the very existence of the Reich.[193]

The chancellor drew an important lesson from the experience of spring 1875: the exposed situation of the new nation state in the heart of Europe could only be protected in the long term by a defensive policy based on the status quo being the most that could be achieved, and linking German interests to the avoidance of a major war. Following this premise, Bismarck developed a new strategy for foreign policy that sought to shift the tensions between the Great Powers to the periphery of Europe, so taking the pressure away from the centre. He was assisted by the great Oriental Crisis of the years 1875 to 1878, which was set off by uprisings among the population of Bosnia and Herzegovina against Turkish rule, and led to a war between Russia and Turkey. Because the German Reich did not have any interests to pursue in the Balkans, a region not 'worth even the healthy bones of a single Pomeranian musketeer', as the chancellor emphasised in a speech to the Reichstag on 5 December 1876,[194] he was now able to try out his new idea of encouraging political rivalries between the Great Powers while at the same time keeping them within certain limits, without the need for the Reich itself to take any risks. This was what he meant when he referred to it as a 'triumph' for German statecraft 'if we manage to keep the oriental ulcer open and so undermine the unity of the other Great Powers and ensure peace for ourselves'.[195]

Bismarck outlined the central idea of this policy in his famous diktat of 15 July 1877, while he was taking the waters at Bad Kissingen. In it, he sketched the idea of an 'overall political situation in which all powers other than France need us, and as far as possible are prevented by their relations with one another from forming coalitions against us'.[196] In fact, Bismarck never managed to attain this ideal configuration of the European powers even while he himself was in office. At the Congress of Berlin in June and July 1878, he presented himself as an 'honest broker' disinterestedly offering his services as mediator and managing the negotiations, but the international regard he afterwards enjoyed as a European statesman was dearly bought. Russia felt it had been cheated of the rewards of its victory over Turkey – above all, of access to the Dardanelles – and it held the Reich chancellor's diplomacy responsible. This was the beginning of the cooling in relations between Russia and Germany, which found its most striking early expression in the 'slap-in-the-face letter' of August 1879 from Alexander II to Wilhelm I; in this letter, the tsar complained that Russia's benevolent neutrality during the Franco-Prussian War had not been duly rewarded. This brought the League of Three Emperors to an end. Once more, the threat of an agreement between Russia and France conjured up the spectre of a war on two fronts. To counter this, Bismarck strove to create closer links with Vienna. In the Dual Alliance of October 1879, Berlin and Vienna guaranteed to support one another in the case of a Russian attack. This defensive treaty evolved an enduring alliance that would only end with the collapse of the two empires in the aftermath of the First World War.

The Dual Alliance was the foundation on which Bismarck built his system of alliances during the 1880s. His calculation that the treaty with Austria-Hungary could be used to bring Russia closer to the German Reich once more paid off. The Three Emperors Treaty was concluded in 1881 after difficult negotiations; in it, the three powers committed themselves to benevolent neutrality should any one of them become involved in a war with another power. In the first instance, this treaty offered security against an alliance between Russia and France for three years. In 1884, it was extended for a further three years and, in 1882, it was supplemented by the Triple Alliance concluded between the German Reich, Austria-Hungary and Italy. This too was a defensive accord with a decidedly anti-French emphasis. In 1883, Romania also joined the Dual Alliance.

Bismarck's admirers have increasingly tended to praise his complex system of alliances as the crowning achievement of his statecraft. But it was more a 'system of expedients'[197] with which the chancellor sought to banish the *cauchemar des coalitions*, the nightmare of a coalition being formed against the Reich, which was slowly becoming a compulsive preoccupation for Bismarck. 'If

Bismarck (left) in the Reichstag circa 1880.

I can claim to have achieved anything of value in foreign policy,'
he explained in a speech to the Reichstag on 14 June 1888, 'it is
that since 1871 I have prevented the formation of any overwhelming coalition against Germany.'[198] In the first half of the 1880s, this
goal really did seem to have been achieved. The German Reich had
become 'the lead weight in a roly-poly doll that keeps making the
figure stand upright again.'[199] That is, it had become a power that
guaranteed peace and the status quo in Europe while at the same
time ensuring that tensions and frictions between the powers on
the periphery continued. The attempt to preserve in the long term a
balance of power so advantageous for Germany turned out to be an
illusory enterprise. At just the moment when Bismarck's system of
treaties seemed to have attained its greatest effectiveness, the newly
emerging colonial epoch introduced a trend that put into question
the doctrine of German 'saturation'. During the 1880s, the call for
colonies became ever louder in Germany too.

At first, Bismarck's attitude to the efforts of the colonial movement was quite reserved. As late as 1881, he affirmed, 'As long as I am chancellor of the Reich, we will not pursue a colonial policy.'[200] But in 1884 and 1885 the Reich abandoned its reserve in colonial policy and took areas in Africa and the South Seas under its protection. There has been much scholarly speculation as to Bismarck's motives for this temporary about-turn, but it has not come to any definitive conclusion.[201] Considerations of domestic and foreign policy were obviously closely entwined. Bismarck seems to have assumed that collaborating in colonial matters would allow him to reduce tensions somewhat in relations with France. On the other hand, he was probably keen to increase the scope for frictions with Britain, above all because of domestic considerations; the chancellor sought to prevent the English sympathies of the crown prince and his wife Victoria, the eldest daughter of Queen Victoria and Prince Albert, from gaining too much influence on German policy in the event of Wilhelm I being succeeded by his son.

Bismarck himself occasionally revealed that he was perturbed by the possibility of a liberal 'Gladstone cabinet', as when in September 1884 he said that the 'single aim of German colonial policy is to drive a wedge between the crown prince and England'.[202] After the fall in March 1885 of the French prime minister, Jules Ferry, who had been inclined to compromise, Bismarck was obliged to give up on the hope of stabilising the European situation of the Reich through a colonial entente with France; after Gladstone's cabinet was replaced by the conservative government of Salisbury in June 1885, he became keener once more on good relations with England. From then on, he lost interest in the colonies. At the beginning of December 1885, he told Eugen Wolf, the German explorer, 'Your map of Africa is indeed very fine, but my map of Africa is in Europe. Here is Russia, and here is France, and we are in the middle; that is my map of Africa.'[203] So colonial policy under Bismarck remained a passing episode, though it was to have lasting consequences. Its results could not be undone, however much the chancellor might wish to distance himself from the 'colonial fraud' that 'made a lubberly mess' of the system of his foreign policy.[204] Overseas 'protectorates' turned into state-run colonies, and these were the embryo of a German colonial empire. This process acquired its own momentum that looked forward to the subsequent 'world politics' of Wilhelm II. Bismarck had thus unintentionally unleashed forces that he himself would eventually be unable to control.

Consolidation and preservation were also the two watchwords for Bismarck's domestic policy after 1871; the situation at first seemed highly promising. On 14 April 1871, the Reichstag passed a new constitution that was largely based on that of the North German Federation; this also meant that Bismarck was confirmed in his dominant position as chancellor of the Reich, Prussian prime minister and foreign minister, and chairman of the Bundesrat. Apart from his constitutional powers, as the founder of the Reich Bismarck had acquired considerable political prestige, and he was able to employ this against Wilhelm I himself in order to get his way. 'It is not easy to be kaiser under such a chancellor', the monarch is once said to have complained.[205] Characterising Bismarck's exceptional position in the Berlin hierarchy, many of his contemporaries spoke of a 'dictatorship of the chancellor'. Drawing on the sociology of Max Weber, Hans-Ulrich Wehler has recently suggested the notion of 'charismatic domination' as the defining feature of Bismarck's rule[206] – an interpretation that has met with criticism, because not all the features of Weber's ideal type are to be found in it. Whatever one's analysis of the role of the Reich chancellor within the power system he created and designed to suit himself, it is certain that he was its lynchpin.

Despite the power Bismarck had concentrated in his own hands, Bismarck was also tormented by anxieties in his domestic policy.

'It is not easy to be kaiser under such a chancellor'. Kaiser Wilhelm I and
Bismarck. Watercolour by Konrad Siemenroth.

He confided to a member of his staff in May 1872, 'My sleep brings no rest, my waking thoughts carry on in my dreams, if I sleep at all. Recently I saw the map of Germany in front of me, and one rotten patch after another appeared and peeled off.'[207]

These anxious visions acquired substance in the great stock market crash of autumn 1873, which brought the long economic boom associated with the foundation of the Reich – the Gründerjahre period– to an abrupt end. There was then an unprecedented fall in share prices and a wave of bankruptcies. The optimism of the Gründerjahre gave way to deep pessimism. The economic liberal belief in the free play of market forces and the blessings of rapid, unlimited growth was shaken to the core. The psychological shock of this crisis gave birth to 'modern' anti-Semitism in Germany. The Jews were identified with speculation and the stock market, now seen as the negative side of the capitalist economic system. Bismarck's private banker, Gerson Bleichröder, found himself more severely exposed to anti-Semitic attacks than almost anyone else. In the eyes of the anti-Semites, he embodied the hated parvenu whose connections with the highest social circles had gained him wealth and power. That Bismarck never found it necessary to publicly defend the man who had done so much for him from these attacks must be seen as one of the darkest pages in his life as a politician.[208]

During the economically difficult years after 1873, which saw severe disruption to growth, Bismarck's tendency to dramatise political conflicts and declare political opponents to be 'enemies of the Reich' increased; he was trying to create other targets for the general disenchantment besides his own government. The first to be affected were the Catholics; after the unification of Germany by Prussia, which was largely Protestant, they suddenly found themselves in the position of a religious minority. The political response to this was that the Catholic population joined together to form the Centre Party, which established itself as the second-largest parliamentary force after the National Liberal Party in the first Reichstag elections in March 1871.

As Bismarck declared in the Reichstag at the end of January 1872, he regarded this new grouping as a 'mobilisation of partisan interests against the state'.[209] Through a series of repressive laws, made constantly more severe from 1872 onwards, he sought to weaken Catholicism as a political force. He particularly hated the spokesman of the Centre Party, Ludwig Windthorst, who gave as good as he got in parliamentary debate against Bismarck. 'My life is preserved and sweetened by two things', Bismarck confessed in January 1875, 'my wife and – Windthorst. One is there for love, and the other for hatred'.[210] But Bismarck had underestimated the power of resistance of the Catholics. The persecution and regulation of their priests only made them more closely united. New forms of intense popular piety became part of the resistance against the attacks of the state. In July 1876, for instance, thousands of pilgrims poured into the village of Morpingen in the Saar, where the Virgin Mary was supposed to have appeared to three girls.[211] Faced with such unexpectedly strong resistance, Bismarck retreated. After 1878, the most severe anti-Catholic laws were gradually withdrawn. Nonetheless, the atmosphere between the Catholics and the Prussian state remained poisonous for a considerable time.

When Bismarck decided to end the 'Kulturkampf' – the government's struggle with the Catholic church for clerical control – he already had another opponent in his sights: Social Democracy. In this case, it was actually easier for him to create an imaginary political danger, because fear of the 'red ghost' had become widespread among the middle class since August Babel, one of the two Social Democrat members of parliament, had expressed his sympathy with the Paris Commune in May 1871. Bismarck pursued a dual strategy against the Social Democratic workers' movement, which remained weak and until 1875 was split into two parties. While repressing the

Bismarck's great enemy of the 1870s, Ludwig Windthorst.

political organisations, he sought to resolve the 'workers' question' by means of progressive social policies.

In practice, it was the repressive half of this approach that was seen at first. After two attacks on Wilhelm I in May and June 1878, which were wrongly laid at the door of the Social Democrats, Bismarck declared during a session of the Privy Council that he wanted to meet Social Democracy with a 'war of annihilation based on laws aimed against the Social Democratic associations and groupings, the press, freedom of movement (by identification and internment)'.[212] This plan was put into effect in the form of the 'Law against the dangerous efforts of Social Democracy' of 21 October 1878. This law, in the severity of repression it allowed, exceeded even the Kulturkampf laws.

But Bismarck's second preventive war on the domestic front also went wrong. It was under the blows of the police and the courts that Social Democracy first became a mass movement, and that a growing number of party members became sympathetic to Marx's theories. Bismarck's attempt to make Social Democracy unattractive to the workers through reforms in social policy remained for the time being ineffective, on the other hand. 'If the workers had no more reason for complaint, the roots of Social Democracy would be cut off', said the chancellor in 1878 in explanation of the aims of his reform initiative.[213] Between 1881 and 1889, laws introducing sickness and accident insurance were passed, and old age and invalidity pensions were introduced. The result was a welfare system that could be regarded as highly progressive for its time; it showed the way into the future insofar as it certainly contributed in the long term to reducing the radical distance and critique of the Social Democratic workers' movement in relation to the Prusso-German authoritarian state.

Bismarck's campaign against Social Democracy coincided with a conservative turn in domestic politics in 1878 and 1879. The beginning was the break with the National Liberal Party, with whose help Bismarck had been able to carry important bills relating to the unification of the economy, administration and legal system through the Reichstag after 1866, and who had also supported him in the Kulturkampf against the Catholics. The chancellor's relationship with political parties was purely instrumental; he used them as long as they could be of use to him, and cast them off as soon as they had performed their function. He dropped the National Liberal Party as soon as it thought of demanding the price of its services to Bismarck: the development of the Reich constitution in a parliamentary direction. This stepped over the mark that Bismarck had set for the party, as he made clear one more time in a speech before the Reichstag on 9 July 1879: 'A parliamentary party can certainly support the government and win some influence over it in return, but if it wants to govern the government, then it compels the government for its part to react.'[214] From then on, the chancellor meant to rely more on the conservative parties and social groups.

This new domestic political situation was reinforced by a fundamental change of direction in economic policy. The liberal, free-trade orientation of the Gründerjahre gave way to a robust protectionism. This change was anticipated in 1876, when heavy industry and large-scale agriculture joined in demanding protective import duties to protect domestic production against the threat of foreign competition. Bismarck, as an estate owner, was particularly concerned for the interests of farmers, but that does not mean he was indifferent to those of industrialists and bankers. He was not, as has frequently been asserted against him, blind to the new world of rapidly developing industrial capitalism; on the contrary, his economic legislation had created optimal conditions for it to flourish. If he now went along with the wishes of the new informal coalition of 'rye and iron', the main reason was that he saw this as an opportunity to commit these two powerful interest groups to the preservation of the existing order, so cementing the conservative foundations of the Lesser German and Greater Prussian state and permanently strengthening the basis of his own power. To do so, he had to accept disadvantages in terms of foreign policy; it was foreseeable that the introduction of the import duties in 1879 would worsen relations with Russia, because its economy was dependent on grain exports to Germany.

Referring to the shift of 1878 and 1879, many historians speak of a 'refoundation' of the Reich.[215] This is surely an exaggeration, for there was no fundamental change in the character of the power structure created in 1871. But it is correct to speak of a change of direction insofar as the end of the 'liberal era' put an end, for the time being, to all moves to make the constitution more progressive. 'Our part seems to be played, and I find I am less and less able to rid myself of the oppressive feeling that I have worked half a lifetime for nothing'[216] – this statement of a left-liberal in January 1880 was typical of the general demoralisation of liberalism in Germany, which was to a considerable extent due to Bismarck. In August 1880, the left wing of the National Liberal Party, led by Eduard Lasker, Max von Forschenbeck and Ludwig Bamberger, left the party and combined with the Progress party to form the German-Freethinking Party. The majority of the National Liberal Party turned to the right, its members committing themselves entirely to preserving the existing political and social order.

The process of liberal decline was a great boon to Bismarck, whose principal concern during the 1880s was to prevent the expected royal succession from precipitating the adoption of a parliamentarian course. Time and time again he declared, 'The creation of a parliamentary regime would in the view of His Majesty's Government certainly lead to the decline and dissolution of the German Reich.'[217] Bismarck's hatred was now focussed on the left-liberals, who would not let go of the idea of a democratic, parliamentarian future for Germany, and above all on Eduard Lasker, whom he saw as the personification of this demand. When Lasker died in 1884 during a visit to the United States, the chancellor refused to pass on a letter of condolence from the American House of Representatives to the Reichstag. Worse still, he forbade members of the government to attend the funeral and abused the dead man in a speech to the Reichstag.[218] Generosity to his political opponents was never Bismarck's strong point, and the fact that Lasker was a Jew may well have added considerably to his dislike.

The less successful that Bismarck was in creating a workable majority in the Reichstag, the more clear his feeling against parties and parliamentarians appeared. After every debate in the Reichstag, he felt 'as if [he] had tussled with the hoi polloi in a dirty pub', he remarked in November 1885.[219] 'I want to defend my king and the kingdom against revolution, whether of the open or surreptitious sort, and I want to create and pass on a healthy, strong Germany. The parties are indifferent to me', was Bismarck's description of his credo for the 1880s.[220] Just as in foreign policy, however, the idea of protecting the existing system against all change, essentially freezing power relations, was an error. At a time when everything was changing – when the dynamic of the industrial-capitalist system of production continued unbroken, despite the susceptibility it had shown to disruptions; when the growth of the railways was proceeding apace; when production of coal, iron and steel was growing at an unheard-of rate; and when more and more people were migrating from the agrarian eastern regions to the industrial areas of the west – at such a time, politics and society could no longer be forced to stand still. Even Bismarck's contemporaries saw his policy of simply preserving the status quo as 'plodding on' without a future, serving only to preserve his own power. Many thought the prescriptions of the ageing chancellor, who had now been at the head of Prussian and German politics for a long time, were exhausted, and it was time for a breath of fresh air. These hopes for change were pinned on to the crown prince; the confirmed liberals expected his ascension to the throne to bring the hated 'Bismarck system' to an end.

The long departure from power 1885–90

> There is no remedy against the approach of old age, and it is
> without joy, but also without bitterness, that I feel my frame
> gradually becoming physically and spiritually more disordered.
> I am tired, and while I am still bound to the life of this world, I
> am starting to sense the appeal of contemplation and rest. What
> I would prefer is to leave the stage for a spectator's box.[221]

Bismarck wrote these words to Katharina Orloff on the first day of
Christmas 1871; in far-off days, she had been the woman he wor-
shipped in Biarritz. He was then fifty-six years old and had been
Reich chancellor of the greatest power on the European continent
for just a few months. He had every reason to be satisfied with his
achievement, yet he felt exhausted. He was never again to be free of
the longing for release from the oppressive burden of official duties.
But Bismarck never did more than toy with the idea of retirement –
he never really entertained it seriously. He was far too enamoured of
power for that, and the passion for politics had conquered him too
utterly, for all that he kept complaining that it had driven his other
interests into the background. 'I often long for repose; but there
can be no repose for me', he said to Robert von Keudell in October
1872.[222] This conflict was to be the leitmotif of his chancellorship,
which lasted nearly another two decades.

Admittedly, Bismarck had to take longer and longer breaks at
Varzin or Friedrichsruh to renew his exhausted strength. 'My oil is

used up, I can do no more', he complained at the beginning of May 1872 before yet again withdrawing from the capital of the Reich for several months.[223] His student friend Motley, who visited him in June 1872 in Varzin, said, 'He looks like a colossus, but his health is really ruined.' [224] Bismarck's constitution indeed remained fragile; at times he suffered from painful facial neuralgias, sometimes from rheumatic complaints or inflammation of the veins in his left leg (the result of his numerous riding accidents years before). He fell victim to digestive troubles and haemorrhoids. But his worst recurrent complaint was insomnia:

> I just can't get to sleep, whatever I try. So I read, get up again, walk around my study, smoke – none of it is of any use, and I often don't get to sleep properly till seven in the morning ... And the shameful thing is that when I cannot get to sleep, I can only think of all the troubles I have had, which seem worse than ever, and never anything pleasant.[225]

Bismarck's poor health was not attributable to his huge workload alone; his imprudent lifestyle also had something to do with it, particularly his immoderate appetite, by which his guests were continually surprised. 'The Prince complains of poor appetite. Hats off! I'd like to see him eat with a good appetite. He takes at least two helpings of each course, and complains of ill treatment when the Princess raises an energetic protest against his partaking of a wild boar's head,' Christoph von Tiedemann exclaimed after his first dinner with the Bismarcks.[226] He had replaced Delbrück as head of the Reich Chancellery in 1875. During the Congress of Berlin in 1875, the British prime minister, Disraeli, observed, 'Prince Bismarck with one hand full of cherries and the other of prawns, which he eats in turn, complains that he cannot sleep and must go to Kissingen.'[227] Bismarck delighted in washing down the

Bismarck at his desk at Friedrichsruh in 1885.

random assortment of food with which he stuffed himself with
several bottles of wine or champagne. The results of this gastro-
nomic excess soon showed themselves, and the chancellor of the
Reich, who had been fairly slim in younger years, became fatter and
fatter, weighing in at 247 pounds in 1879.

In 1883, a young Bavarian doctor, Ernst Schweninger, took on the treatment of this difficult patient, and he managed to put a stop to the excess. He prescribed a diet for Bismarck, limited his consumption of alcohol and tobacco and induced him to take regular exercise in the fresh air. This regime was effective, and from then on Bismarck's health visibly improved. 'He is the only person in my entire life who has gained power over me and to whom I render almost unconditional obedience', Bismarck said of Schweninger.[228]

Even more than from his health, the ageing chancellor suffered from increasing isolation. His former conservative confidants had gradually turned away from him. 'At sixty one makes no new friends and I have lost the old ones', he repeatedly complained during the 1870s.[229] More and more, Bismarck withdrew into his immediate family, where he knew Johanna would tend to him like a mother; even there, he made a somewhat odd impression. A friend of the family, the Baroness of Spitzemberg, observed in 1885, 'There is something self-contained in him in the circle of his wife and children.'[230] Of his three children, he was closest to his elder son, Herbert. At his father's wish, Herbert entered the diplomatic service in 1874, and twelve years later he became one of the chancellor's closest assistants as the state secretary of the Foreign Office. But in 1881 the two almost broke with one another when Bismarck forbade his son to marry Princess Elizabeth von Carolath, a divorcee ten years older, even threatening suicide. Herbert bowed to his father's command and remained thereafter an embittered man.[231]

Though Bismarck could be genial enough in a small social circle, he was suspicious of subordinates and political rivals. He scented intrigues and conspiracies in every quarter. Anyone he suspected of having his own ambitions to hold the office of chancellor was quickly shunted off into political limbo. Bismarck basically thought he was indispensable, so he did not give any thought to his possible successor, not even admitting that anyone could fit the bill. 'At all costs he wants to remain possible, now and in future, and this is probably because he feels the building he has begun will collapse amidst the scornful laughter of the whole world as soon as he takes his hand away,' the war minister, Roon, had written as early as January 1870 to Moritz von Blankenburg,[232] and the same was true fifteen years later. It was as if Bismarck wanted to make his chancellorship permanent. But at the end of the 1880s, the signs that his time was up began to grow.

First of all, the delicate web of Bismarck's system of treaties was subjected to a severe test. After renewed upsets in the Balkans in 1884 and 1885, during the course of which tensions between Austria-Hungary and Russia reached a dangerous pitch, the Three Emperors Treaty of 1881 collapsed. With the Reinsurance Treaty concluded on 18 June 1887, Bismarck sought to tie Russia once more to the German Reich. In a 'completely secret supplementary protocol', he guaranteed Russia German support if it should feel compelled to take possession of the 'keys of its empire', the access to the Dardanelles. This concession certainly conflicted with the Mediterranean Entente concluded in February and March 1887 with Britain, Italy and Austria-Hungary, which Bismarck had worked hard to bring about. This accord was directed above all against Russian efforts to encroach on the Balkans, particularly the Russian aim of gaining control of the Dardanelles. Bismarck consciously accepted this conflict in the hope of being able to hold in balance the rival interests of the other powers as before, thus preserving the threatened peace.

Meanwhile, public criticism in Germany of his diplomacy became ever more vociferous. A widespread feeling at the end of the 1880s was that, instead of restricting itself to preserving the status quo, the German Reich should conduct a foreign policy in keeping with its economic strength, without being put off by the risk of a war. The idea of a pre-emptive war gained more and more ground among diplomats and the military. 'Practically everyone here is in favour of war', reported the privy counsellor at the Foreign Office,

The future Kaiser Friedrich III and Empress Victoria shortly after their marriage in 1858.

Friedrich von Holstein, in January 1888, 'almost the only exception being His Excellency, who is making the utmost effort to preserve the peace.'[233] In domestic matters, Bismarck had taken ruthless preventive action against supposed threats, but when it came to foreign policy he absolutely rejected the idea of a pre-emptive war, in which he was convinced the German Reich stood to gain nothing and might indeed lose everything. At the close of 1887, he summed up his position once more: 'Our policy has the task of completely avoiding war if possible; if not, it should postpone it.'[234]

A few months later, on 9 March 1888, the long-expected event occurred: Kaiser Wilhelm I died at the age of almost ninety-one, and Crown Prince Friedrich Wilhelm ascended the throne as Friedrich III. Bismarck had made preparations for this moment in order to make himself indispensable and a change in the direction of domestic policy impossible. But if Friedrich III ever thought of setting a truly different course, in the direction of a liberal parliamentary system on English lines, he had no opportunity to do so; by the time he was finally able to succeed to the throne, he was already mortally ill, and he reigned for only ninety-nine days.

Once Bismarck learned of Friedrich's untreatable cancer of the throat, his concerns turned to the kaiser's eldest son, Prince Wilhelm. Though he certainly could not be suspected of having liberal tendencies, Wilhelm was unmistakably a member of a thrusting new generation of grandsons, to whom the comparatively aged founder of the Reich must seem almost like a prehistoric figure. Even before ascending the throne as Wilhelm II, he made it clear that he wanted to take the reins of power into his own hands, unlike his grandfather. Bismarck's impression, for his part, that the 'young master' was still very immature and insufficiently prepared for his high office was already confirmed in his eyes by the end of 1887. He complained to a visitor to Friedrichsruh that Prince Wilhelm was 'a hothead, could not hold his tongue, was susceptible to flatterers, and was capable of plunging Germany into a war without knowing what he was doing'.[235]

With two such different men at the helm of the Reich, conflict was inevitable. Bismarck must have recognised the danger in which the exaggerated self-confidence and impetuous temperament of the young monarch placed him. To counter the impending threat of loss of power, he turned to an apparently tried-and-tested recipe, namely stoking up domestic political conflicts by polarising the situation so that the kaiser would be left with no alternative but to call on the support of the chancellor, with all his experience of defusing crises. At the end of October 1889, he introduced a draft bill to the Reichstag for a new, more severe Socialist Law, which – unlike the old one that expired in autumn 1889 – was to be valid permanently. This proposal was an explosive attack on the 'Cartel', the majority formed by the two conservative parties and the National Liberal Party; it had supported the government since the Reichstag elections of 1887. It was known that the National Liberal Party would not vote for a more severe version of the Socialist Law. 'The Reich chancellor is driving us into a serious conflict, and he no longer has the strength corresponding to his earlier authority to master it', Grand Duke Friedrich I of Baden recognised at the end of November 1889.[236]

But Wilhelm II would not let Bismarck force him down the path of conflict in domestic politics. On the contrary, he wanted to open his reign with a conciliatory gesture. To this end, he considered an ambitious programme to improve welfare provision for workers – going beyond Bismarck's social insurance laws. At a session of the Privy Council on 24 January 1890, the conflict between these opposed viewpoints came to a head. Wilhelm II demanded that the draft of the new Socialist Law be toned down, whereas Bismarck bluntly rejected all compromise, arguing that if the kaiser 'was of a different opinion in such an important matter, then he himself was probably no longer the right man for his job', and that if the law collapsed in the Reichstag, 'we would have to make do without it, and let the waves rise higher'. But the monarch rejected any thought of violent action against Social Democracy; he 'did not want to stain the first years of his reign with the blood of his subjects'.[237]

Those present at the Privy Council left it with the feeling that, as one of them wrote the same day, 'an irreparable breach had occurred between the chancellor and the Sovereign'. In fact, it was to be almost another two months before Bismarck handed in his letter of resignation on 18 March. The intervening weeks were occupied by ever more desperate attempts on the part of the chancellor to remain in power. He did not shrink from seriously considering the idea of a coup d'état, which he had threatened from time to time in the 1860s and 1870s. In the session of the Prussian Staatsministe-rium that took place on 2 March 1890, he developed a scenario for a coup: as the alliance on which the constitution was based had been concluded by sovereign rulers, the latter could 'if necessary' decide to withdraw 'multilaterally from their joint accord'. The draft of the minutes contained an addition at this point that Bismarck crossed out, clearly because it made his purposes all too transparent: 'In this way it would be possible to free ourselves of the Reichstag, if the elections continued to turn out badly.'[238]

But, as ever, even in this extreme situation, Bismarck was juggling with several options. On 12 March, for instance, he sounded out his former bosom enemy Ludwig Windthorst, the leader of the Centre Party, on the possibility of forming a new parliamentary majority based on a conservative-clerical alliance. Immediately after their dis-cussion, Windthorst said, 'I have come from the political deathbed of a great man.'[239] But none of Bismarck's political stratagems was any use. On 15 March, Wilhelm II drew a line under the months-long power struggle. In an emotional statement, he ruled out any support for the chancellor's confrontational programme – amounting to

'Dropping the Pilot'. The famous cartoon by Sir John Tenniel
published in *Punch* in March 1890.

inviting his resignation. Bismarck spent two days polishing his resignation letter. It was a final masterpiece, so skilfully composed that all
the responsibility for the split was laid at the kaiser's door. Bismarck
deliberately brought foreign policy into it, although this had not
played a decisive role in the crisis. Wilhelm II – the letter implied
– sought a different policy, inclined to war, which he, the chancellor, could not serve. It had now become apparent to him, Bismarck
ended the letter, that the kaiser no longer needed the 'experience
and abilities of a true servant of his ancestors'; he could resign
without needing to fear that this decision 'would be condemned by
public opinion as premature.'[240]
Many sections of the German public were in fact relieved at

Bismarck's fall. 'It's for the best that we are rid of him,' commented the writer Theodor Fontane. 'Really, he was no longer anything but the ruler we were used to; he did what he wanted while demanding ever more devotion. His greatness lay behind him.'[241] This was a typical sentiment. It seemed that an era of crippling stagnation was coming to an end. Abroad, however, where Bismarck was seen as the guarantor of peaceful foreign policy, the news was met with concern. 'Here, people still can't quite take in the thought that the great man who has led our political life for the past quarter century is to make way for someone else,' reported the German ambassador in St Petersburg, Albert von Pourtalès.[242]

Bismarck retreated discontentedly to Friedrichsruh. The public send-off he received when he left Berlin on 29 March was, he felt, 'a first-class funeral procession'.[243] His departure from power was a cold one. Anything else was hardly to be expected in the case of a man who had only ever used others like chess pieces and had not allowed any political figures of character to develop alongside him. Baroness von Spitzemberg prophesied:

> As for the Bismarck family, they will be overcome by the nemesis they deserve for the brutality and ruthlessness with which they trod so many people, great and small, into the dust; but it will not be a pleasant sight. My God, the meanness that will show itself now, after the Byzantine fawning of former days![244]

The last years 1890–8

Those who hoped Bismarck would put himself completely out to grass after his dismissal were soon put right. The fallen chancellor, for whom politics had become central to life, had no intention of practising restraint in future. As he declared in May 1890, 'They can't expect me to suddenly leave off politics after being involved in it for forty years.'[245] Even in the first few weeks after his fall, he expressed very definite opinions in numerous interviews. He also formed close links with a few newspapers that were politically sympathetic to him, especially the *Hamburger Nachrichten*, whose proprietor, Emil Hartmeyer, offered during a visit to Friedrichsruh on 15 April 1890 to place the paper entirely at the service of the former chancellor; the paper's political editor, Hermann Hofmann, effectively became Bismarck's mouthpiece. Hofmann was a journalist without scruples, and he allowed Bismarck to pay off his debts in return for the use of his agile pen.[246] Naturally, it would not do for the direct control of the Hamburg paper from Friedrichsruh to be too apparent, and so Bismarck took a certain amount of care to disguise the articles inspired by him as the expression of editorial opinion.

The ex-chancellor's journalistic campaigns targeted his successor, Leo von Caprivi, at first with some restraint, but then ever more outspokenly. One of his first official acts was the decision not to renew the Reinsurance Treaty with Russia. Bismarck thought that the advocates of the 'new course' were threatening his entire achievement in foreign policy, and he lost no opportunity to warn repeatedly against the danger of the Reich becoming isolated. Of course, in this he was gambling on the short memories of his contemporaries; the cooling of relations between the Reich and Russia was not just the result of Caprivi's change of policy, but had begun while Bismarck was still chancellor.

Ultimately, the attacks on Caprivi were aimed at the kaiser. Bismarck had no intention of forgiving him for casting him off 'like a servant: all my life, I have felt the presence of a nobleman within me who cannot be insulted with impunity'.[247] Johanna did all she could to provoke her husband's hatred: 'The age of Methuselah would not be enough to sit out the prison sentences that my wife makes herself liable for every day through treasonable utterances', Bismarck once half-jokingly said.[248]

In the kaiser's circle, it was feared that Bismarck was attempting a political comeback and possibly even intended to put himself at the head of a movement calling for a plebiscite. Such speculation received a boost in March 1891, when Bismarck decided – to general surprise – to accept an offer to stand for the National Liberal Party in a Reichstag by-election for a Hanover constituency. Bismarck defeated the Social Democrat candidate in the vote at the end of April, but then failed to take up his seat. It would hardly have been conceivable, given that he had never concealed his contempt for the parliamentarians, for him to take his place among them as a mere member of parliament. But the very idea that he might turn up in Berlin in a situation of internal political conflict, 'like Banquo's ghost at Macbeth's table',[249] was enough to generate a state of alarm in government circles in the capital of the Reich, for an incredible turnaround in the public estimation of Bismarck had now begun, and since his dismissal his reputation had risen again; it increased as his opponents – led by the kaiser – began to attack him openly.

The growing idolisation of the former chancellor was a political fact of great importance, because it made all the clearer the distance

Wilhelm II and Bismarck at Friedrichsruh.

that separated the founder of the Reich, who had become a national father figure, from his comparatively mediocre successors. Wilhelm II's self-confidence as a monarch must have been profoundly shaken by the fact that another man enjoyed greater popularity among the people than did he himself.

There was a sensation in summer 1892, when Bismarck's intention to travel to Vienna for the long-delayed wedding of his son Herbert with Marguerite Hoyos was revealed. In Berlin, it was suspected that a carefully prepared political coup of some kind lay behind the plan. Accordingly, the kaiser and his chancellor reacted with panic. Caprivi instructed the German ambassador in Vienna, Prince Reuss, to avoid accepting any invitation to the wedding, and Wilhelm II suggested that Kaiser Franz Josef I of Austria should not grant an audience to his 'disobedient subject'.[250] None of this could do anything to prevent the ex-chancellor from receiving the ovations of the public wherever he made a stop on his journey – in Dresden, Vienna, Munich, Bad Kissingen. In an interview with the *Neue Freie Presse* in Vienna, Bismarck gave vent to his resentment by declaring – for the benefit of Berlin – that he had 'absolutely no further personal responsibility' to his successors: 'All bridges are broken.'[251]

Wilhelm II gradually came to realise that the state of war with Friedrichsruh was extremely damaging to his public standing, and in the end he summoned Bismarck to a meeting in Berlin. The encounter of 26 January 1894 was presented as a great moment of reconciliation between monarch and ex-chancellor and was greeted with public enthusiasm. 'It was as if we were all carried aloft by the great hope, free at last of the oppressively divided feeling for the kaiser and for the founder of the German Reich,' observed Baroness von Spitzemberg.[252] On 19 February 1894, Wilhelm II made a reciprocal visit to Bismarck at Friedrichsruh; the feud seemed to be at an end. But there could be no question of reconciliation. Bismarck's contemptuous view of the young kaiser had not changed in the slightest, and for Wilhelm II the over-powerful shadow of the 'old man in the Saxon Forest' remained a constant irritation.

In autumn 1896, Bismarck once more provoked consternation when he revealed the secret of the Reinsurance Treaty with Russia in the *Hamburger Nachrichten*. This was an extraordinary act that created shockwaves in Germany and abroad. In his first fury, Wilhelm II declared that he wanted to have Bismarck incarcerated at Spandau Prison for treason. The monarch then took revenge in his own way in a speech to the provincial parliament of Branden- burg on 26 February 1867, by immoderately praising his grandfather Wilhelm I and writing off his advisers, above all Bismarck, as mere 'lackeys' and 'pygmies'. 'The old man in his modesty would turn over in his grave,' was Baron von Spitzemberg's comment on this rhetori- cal faux pas.[253]

In his last years, Bismarck became increasingly isolated, despite his growing cult of personality. Johanna died on 27 September 1894 at the age of seventy, and he bore the loss hard: 'What was left to me was Johanna, spending time with her, the daily question of her contentment, the sense of thankfulness with which I look back over forty-eight years. And today everything is bare and empty', he wrote to his sister three weeks later.[254] The numerous declarations of gratitude and respect that were delivered to him on the occasion of his eightieth birthday on 1 April 1895 overcame once more his feeling of resignation, but, in a free vote on 23 March 1895, the Reichstag had declined to send Bismarck a congratulatory address. This was a clear indication of how deep-seated the bitterness of a majority of the parliamentarians remained over his policy of confrontation in domestic politics.

From 1896 on, Bismarck's health declined rapidly. As well as painful facial neuralgias, he suffered from problems of circulation in his left leg. Phases of extreme irritability alternated with lengthy depressions. 'He suffered from living,' wrote the journalist Maximilian Harden, 'he suffered unutterably from the knowledge that his bodily powers were deserting his restlessly active mind.'[255] Bismarck now hardly left his wheelchair – not even when Wilhelm II visited him one last time on 16 December 1897 and entertained the embarrassed company with barrack-room jokes. 'Your Majesty, as long as you have this corps of officers, you can naturally permit yourself everything; but should that no longer be the case, things will be quite different', said Bismarck prophetically, when there was a pause.[256] Slowly but unstoppably, his will to live was extinguished. On 30 July 1898, at around 11 p.m., Otto von Bismarck died. One of his last wishes was, 'Grant that I may see my Johanna once again.'[257]

Assessment

On the news of Bismarck's death, the young theatre critic Alfred Kerr wrote:

> A shivering and trembling comes over you – even if you don't want it to. Even for someone whose basic feeling was a kind of hatred for the man, at this moment you feel how deeply you loved him, albeit discontentedly. A piece of Germany has sunk beneath the waves of history for all eternity. Farewell.[258]

Many people felt that Bismarck's death marked the end of an epoch; it was only now that the cult of his personality lost all proportion. Bismarck had stated before he died, 'I have never placed much value in titles and decorations, nor in the monuments that have been erected in my honour, or are proposed. I do not want to be a spectacle, nor do I wish to see myself turned to stone, or mummified while I am still alive.'[259] But this wish was not respected. After 1898, Bismarck monuments sprang out of the ground like mushrooms. They showed the founder of the Reich as a statesman in uniform, complete with pickelhaube helmet, jackboots and sabre – a knight in armour, a sort of King Arthur of the Reich, gazing into the far distance with a grim expression.[260]

The Bismarck myth rapidly lost touch with the real historical figure. Behind the monumental image of the 'Iron Chancellor', the defining characteristic of Bismarck's foreign policy since the mid-1870s was lost from view – namely his sense for moderation and restraint arising from the insight that the German Reich could only be preserved if it defined itself as 'saturated'. Time and again, he warned that the first priority was to secure 'what we have laboriously achieved under threat of armed attack by the rest of Europe'.[261] It was a message that was heeded less and less towards the end of his rule, let alone after his dismissal in 1890.

The young generation, anxious to follow the seductive call of 'world politics', felt that his policy of pursuing balance to assure the peace was out of date. Harry Graf Kessler, who as part of a student delegation presented Bismarck with an honorary trophy in Bad Kissingen in 1891, was disappointed:

> The longer we listened, the clearer it became to us that what he was saying was directed at a generation that belonged to the past ... He offered us young Germans the goal of defending and enjoying what had already been gained, politically speaking the existence of a pensioner; no satisfaction for our desire to do great things ... As was painfully obvious, it was not a beginning but an end, a grandiose closing chord – a fulfiller, not a prophet![262]

Yet that was just what Bismarck became after his death – the figurehead of an overheated nationalism onto whom vague imperialistic longings could be projected. In the process, one of his key maxims was forgotten: that politics should always remain the 'art of the possible', or as he sometimes also expressed it, 'a science of the possible'.[263] In everything that Bismarck planned and carried out as a politician, he had adapted seamlessly to prevailing situations, calculating how best to take advantage of them to achieve his ends. He had a greater influence than any other man on the fate of Germany and Europe in the nineteenth century, yet he was always conscious of the limits to his political actions. 'One thing you learn

Memorial statue to Bismarck in Baden-Baden.

thoroughly in this business is that you can be as clever as anyone in this world, and still at any moment you may find yourself walking in the dark like a child', he wrote to his wife after his first foreign policy triumph during the July 1864 Schleswig-Holstein dispute.[264] This was not false modesty – Bismarck never suffered from a lack of self-confidence – but an expression of his deep-seated scepticism when it came to the notion of planning and making history. 'One cannot oneself create anything; one can only wait till one hears the footsteps of God resounding through events; then leap forward and seize hold of the hem of his coat – that is all.'[265]

And that was a great deal! The ability to wait for the decisive instant, taking advantage of a uniquely favourable moment with determination – this was a skill Bismarck honed to the point of perfection. That is why he was once described, not without reason, as a 'genius of the present';[266] in this he differed from the succeeding generation of Wilhelmine politicians. The one thing they could not do was wait, and their hectic activism led the Reich into international isolation.

One of the striking contradictions that characterise Bismarck's life's work and make him such a fascinating politician is that, though he did so much to shape his times, he was filled with a lasting feeling of impotence against the great forces by which history is shaped. 'For a man cannot create and direct the current of time', he lectured even after his fall, 'he can only travel down it and steer, with more or less experience and skill; he may be shipwrecked, or run aground, or he may come into safe harbours'.[267]

In the end, it almost amounted to a self-fulfilling prophecy that Bismarck, having made use of the dominant forces of his time with such mastery, was no longer able to keep them under control. The dynamic of industrial capitalism – which, in the context of the Lesser German and Greater Prussian nation state created by Bismarck, was better able to develop than previously – undermined his status quo policy, and with a certain inner logic encouraged his successors to follow the path of imperialist expansion. It was a misinterpretation of Bismarck's intentions to claim him for the new magic formula of 'world politics', though the chancellor of the Reich may have lent credence to this misunderstanding through his passing flirtation with the colonial movement.

The mythologisation of the former chancellor also disguised the heavy burdens that were the legacy of his domestic policy. Bismarck's inclination to stir up sociopolitical conflicts and polarise them into an opposition between friend and enemy introduced an element of violence into domestic politics that permanently poisoned the political culture of the Reich. 'He who is with me is my friend, he who goes against me is my enemy – to the point of annihilation,' he confessed to a National Liberal Party politician in 1878, the year of the conservative turn.[268] First the Catholics and then the Social Democrats found out just how seriously he meant this. It was above all the latter that he persecuted with bitter hatred. 'They are rats overrunning the country, and must be destroyed', he stated in an interview with an American journalist in 1893.[269] This rhetoric of annihilation derived from his fear of a revolution, that *cauchemar des révolutions* that was matched in his foreign policy after 1871 by the *cauchemar des coalitions*. Bismarck never forgot the traumatic experience of the revolution of 1848, when he had seen the whole political and social order in which he had grown up and from which his sense of identity derived placed under threat. After 1866, his domestic policy was dominated by the idea of preventing any situation that might make possible a repetition of the events of March 1848.

Bismarck's exclusion of those with different political views as 'enemies of the Reich', the gagging of parliament and political parties, the subordination of the press, the reactionary makeup of the civil service, his flirtation with the idea of a coup, and finally his anti-Semitic prejudices – these were burdens that were to have fateful consequences for German politics. Theodor Mommsen's verdict in old age was that Bismarck had 'broken the nation's backbone'. The harm caused by his period in power was 'greater by far than its benefits, for the gains in power were lost once more when the next world-historical storm arose. But the enslavement of the German character, the German mind, was a curse that could not be undone.'[270]

In 1917, in the third year of the Great War, when the Reich was already rapidly approaching its end, the sociologist Max Weber commented on 'the inheritance of Bismarck' in similar terms: the founder of the Reich 'desired ... and promoted the political impotence of parliament and party politics'; he was unable 'to tolerate any power alongside himself, of whatever nature, that was in any way independent, that is, that acted on its own responsibility'. The result was that 'he left behind a nation without any political culture whatsoever, far below the level it had already reached in this respect twenty years before. Above all, it was a nation without any political will whatsoever, accustomed to politics being taken care of on its behalf by the great statesman at its head.' Weber saw this authoritarian and hierarchical fixation as 'by far the worst harm' caused by the age of Bismarck.[271]

As early as 1887, the liberal Georg von Bunsen had lamented, 'Bismarck makes Germany great, and the Germans small.'[272] This has remained the tone of liberal critique of Bismarck, from Mommsen and Weber to the three-volume biography (1941–4) by Erich Eyck. Justified as this critique is, the question remains whether the liberals themselves did not have a share of the responsibility for the negative consequences of Bismarck's rule. Can it not be said that they made things easy for the chancellor by making themselves smaller than they actually were?

Ludwig Bamberger, who was in a position to know, commented self-critically at the end of the century that Bismarck had only been able to get the better of parliament because he recognised the 'political immaturity of the German middle class', which did not face him with a strength sufficient to compel him to take account of its demands.[273] This verdict was certainly not without justification. Blinded by Bismarck's successes from 1864 to 1866, most liberals had quite unnecessarily followed 'the mistaken course of surrender'[274] and subordinated their liberal demands for freedom to the cause of national unity. Bismarck took advantage of their ready submissiveness when, after the foundation of the German Federation, he at first worked with the National Liberal Party and then dropped it once he had no more need of it, after first having contributed much to the demoralisation and division of the party. 'When the great chancellor finally retires,' General von Schweinitz, who served as German ambassador to the tsar's court for many years, prophesied in the 1880s, 'many people will be ashamed and reproach one another with their spinelessness in bowing to his mighty will.'[275] This was no doubt also true of the bulk of the National Liberal Party.

As Lothar Gall has remarked, to a sober eye the Reich created by Bismarck appears 'to be an extremely unstable and short-lived formation'.[276] In 1918, after the First World War – provoked by Wilhelmine Germany – the Hohenzollern monarchy was compelled to leave the stage of world history; in 1945, after the Second World War, the first German nation state was destroyed for ever. Ever since, historians have considered again and again whether the seeds of this catastrophic end were already present at the foundation of the Reich in 1871. Simple answers – such as the view that Bismarck was the 'first demon' in recent German history, whose hubris gave birth directly to the second, Adolf Hitler[277] – are erroneous. Though the burdens that Bismarck left his heirs were a heavy debt, failure and collapse were certainly not the inevitable consequences. To be sure, Bismarck made every effort to permanently cement the conservative basis of the Prusso-German monarchy, and to prevent the system he had created from developing in a liberal and parliamentary direction, but these structures were not so solid as to exclude all possibility of a change of course. The blame for the failure to use the available opportunities can no longer be laid at Bismarck's door.

A century after the founder of the Reich was dismissed, the two partial German states that had arisen from the insolvent estate of the Third Reich were reunited. Does this mean Bismarck has now gained an 'almost oppressive significance'?[278] Certainly not. The second German nation state has almost nothing in common with the first. It arose not out of wars, but from peaceful negotiations with the victorious powers of the Second World War. Rather than destroying the European balance of power, it has taken its place in a Europe that has grown more strongly united. In its internal constitution, it is the exact opposite of the authoritarian system that Bismarck called into being and ruthlessly defended. Perhaps it can be said that this controversial statesman now, for the first time, belongs wholly to history – and for that reason we can judge him, with all his limitations and achievements, more impartially than was possible for earlier generations.

Notes

Key to abbreviated forms for frequently cited works:

Busch 1–3 Moritz Busch, *Tagebuchblätter* Vols. 1–3 (Leipzig: 1899).

Keudell Robert von Keudell, *Fürst und Fürstin Bismarck. Erinnerungen aus den Jahren 1846 bis 1872* (Berlin-Stuttgart: 1901).

Letters Herbert Bismarck (ed.), *Fürst Bismarcks Briefe an seine Braut und Gattin* (Stuttgart: 1900).

Works Otto von Bismarck, *Die Gesammelten Werke. Friedrichsruher Ausgabe*, 15 volumes expanded to 19 volumes (Berlin: 1924–35).

Speeches Horst Kohl (ed.), *Die politischen Reden des Fürsten Bismarck 1847–1897* 14 vols (Stuttgart: 1892–1905).

1. Busch 3, p 276.
2. Cf. Christoph Studt, *Lothar Bucher (1817–1892). Ein politisches Leben zwischen Revolution und Staatsdienst* (Göttingen: 1992) pp 320ff.
3. Busch 3, p 330.
4. Rudolf Vierhaus (ed.), *Das Tagebuch der Baronin Spitzemberg. Aufzeichnungen aus der Hofgesellschaft des Hohenzollernreiches* (5th ed., Göttingen: 1989) p 381.

5. Heinrich Poschinger (ed.), *Fürst Bismarck. Neue Tischgespräche und Interviews* Vol. 2 (Stuttgart–Leipzig: 1899) p 419.

6. In this vein, Johannes Willms, *Bismarck – Dämon der Deutschen. Anmerkungen zu einer Legende* (Munich: 1977).

7. Lothar Gall, *Bismarck. Der weiße Revolutionär* (Frankfurt am Main–Berlin–Vienna: 1980) (cited according to the pagination of the 1983 paperback ed.).

8. Ernst Engelberg, *Bismarck. Urpreuße und Reichsgründer* (Berlin: 1985); Ernst Engelberg, Bismarck. *Das Reich in der Mitte Europas* (Berlin: 1990), hereafter Engelberg, *Bismarck*.

9. Otto Pflanze, *Bismarck. Der Reichsgründer*; Otto Pflanze, Bismarck. *Der Reichskanzler* (Munich: 1997–8).

10. Keudell, p 220f.

11. Quoted from Hans-Joachim Schoeps, *Bismarck über Zeitgenossen – Zeitgenossen über Bismarck* (Frankfurt am Main–Berlin–Vienna: 1981) p 10.

12. Bismarck to Leopold von Gerlach, 2–4 May 1860; *Works* 14, p 549.

13. Quoted from Erich Marcks, *Bismarck. Eine Biographie 1815–1851* (Berlin: 1939) p 31f.

14. Cf. Engelberg, *Bismarck* Vol. 1, pp 61, 103.

15. Hedwig von Bismarck, *Erinnerungen aus dem Leben einer 95 jährigen* (Halle: 1910) p 30.

16. *Letters*, p 65.

17. Quotations: Keudell, p 160f (18 Jan 1864); Busch 2, p 22 (8 Jan 1871); Robert Freiherr Lucius von Ballhausen, *Bismarck-Erinnerungen* (Stuttgart–Berlin: 1920) p 85.

18. Charlotte Sempell, 'Unbekannte Briefstellen Bismarcks', *Historische Zeitschrift* 207 (1968) pp 609f, 611f, hereafter Sempell, 'Unbekannte Briefstellen'.

19. Quoted from Marcks, *Bismarck. Eine Biographie*, p 51.

20. Facsimile in Christian Graf von Krockow, *Bismarck* (Stuttgart: 1997) p 25, hereafter Krockow.

21. Marcks, *Bismarck. Eine Biographie*, p 53.

22. Krockow, p 25.

23. *Works* 15, p 5.

24. *Works* 15, p 6.

25. Busch 2, p 276.

26. *Vom jungen Bismarck. Briefwechsel Otto von Bismarcks mit Gustav Scharlach* (Weimar: 1912) p 6.

27. Cf. Marcks, *Bismarck. Eine Biographie*, p 80.

28. Graf Alexander Keyserling, *Ein Lebensbild aus seinen Briefen und Tagebüchern* Vol. 1 (Berlin: 1902) p 547.

29. Bismarck to Scharlach, 18 Jun 1835, *Works* 14, p 6.

30. Marcks, *Bismarck. Eine Biographie*, p 110.

31. Quoted from Engelberg, *Bismarck* Vol. 1, p 134.

32. Engelberg, *Bismarck* Vol. 1, p 136.

33. Engelberg, *Bismarck* Vol. 1, p 140.

34. Engelberg, *Bismarck* Vol. 1, p 143.

35. Quoted from Gall, *Bismarck. Der weiße Revolutionär*, p 38.

36. Bismarck to Scharlach, 9 Jan 1845, *Works* 14, p 30.

37. *Works* 14, p 15.

38. Gall, *Bismarck. Der weiße Revolutionär*, p 43f.

39. Letter to Johanna, 15 Feb 1847, Sempell, 'Unbekannte Briefstellen', p 610.

40. Pflanze, *Bismarck* Vol. 1, p 62.

41. Letter to von Klitzing, 10 Sep 1843, Marcks, *Bismarck. Eine Biographie*, p 166.

42. Bismarck to Scharlach, 9 Jan 1845, *Works* 14, p 31.

43. Marie von Thadden to Moritz von Blankenburg, 7 Feb 1843, *Bismarck. Eine Biographie*, p 208.

44. Marcks, *Bismarck. Eine Biographie*, p 228.

45. Marcks, *Bismarck. Eine Biographie*, p 209.

46. Bismarck to Heinrich von Puttkamer, 21 Dec 1846, *Works* 14, p 47.

47. Arnold Oskar Meyer, *Bismarcks Glaube im Spiegel der "Loosungen und Lehrtexte"* (Munich: 1933) p 16, hereafter Meyer, *Bismarcks Glaube*.

48. *Works* 14, p 46.

49. Bismarck to his brother Bernhard, 31 Jan 1847, *Works* 14, p 50 (also for the following quotation).

50. *Letters*, p 18 (7 Feb 1847).

51. Cf. The sensitive portrait by Waltraut Engelberg, *Otto und Johanna von Bismarck* (Berlin: 1990), especially p 98f.

52. *Letters*, p 226 (4 Jan 1851).

53. Cf. Hans-Christoph Kraus, *Ernst Ludwig von Gerlach, Politisches Denken und Handeln eines preußischen Altkonservativen* Vol. 1 (Göttingen: 1994) pp 352ff.

54. *Speeches* 1, p 10.

55. *Letters*, p 90 (18 May 1847).

56. *Speeches* 1, pp 23, 26.

57. *Letters*, p 103 (15 Jun 1847).

58. Cf. Fritz Stern, *Gold und Eisen. Bismarck und sein Bankier Bleichröder* (Reinbek bei Hamburg: 1988), hereafter Stern, *Gold und Eisen*.

59. *Letters*, p 89 (18 May 1847). Also for the following quotation.

60. *Denkwürdigkeiten aus dem Leben des Generalfeldmarschalls Kriegsministers Grafen Roon* Vol. 1 (Berlin: 1905) p 142, hereafter Roon, *Denkwürdigkeiten*.

61. *Works* 15, p 19.

62. Cf. Augusta's undated sketch of 1862, printed in facsimile in Egmont Zechlin, *Bismarck und die Grundlegung der deutschen Großmacht* (2nd ed., Darmstadt: 1960) after p 254; Bismarck's account in 'Erinnerungen und Gedanken',

Works 15, p 29 f; and, for an evaluation of the sources, Gall, *Bismarck. Der weiße Revolutionär*, p 70f.

63. Quoted from Schoeps, *Bismarck über Zeitgenossen – Zeitgenossen über Bismarck*, p 32 (see p 31f. for Bismarck's further statements on Augusta).

64. *Works* 15, p 32.

65. *Speeches* 1, p 46.

66. *Letters,* p 111.

67. Bismarck to L. von Gerlach, 7 Jul 1848, *Works* 14, p 109.

68. Keudell, p 20.

69. Quoted from Marcks, *Bismarck. Eine Biographie*, p 467.

70. Ernst Ludwig von Gerlach, Jakob von Gerlach (ed.), *Aufzeichnungen aus seinem Leben und Wirken 1795–1877* Vol. 2: 1848–1877 (Schwerin: 1903) p 27 (11 Nov 1848).

71. Friedrich Ferdinand Graf von Beust, *Aus drei Vierteljahrhunderten. Erinnerungen und Aufzeichnungen* Vol. 1: 1809–1866 (Stuttgart: 1887) p 50.

72. *Letters,* p 122 (17 Nov 1848).

73. Ballhausen, *Bismarck-Erinnerungen*, p 20 (14 Apr 1872).

74. As Bismarck wrote to his brother, Bernhard, 18 Apr 1849, *Works* 14, p 127.

75. *Speeches* 1, p 94.

76. Conversation with Hermann Wagener, 9 Jun 1848, *Works* 7, p 13.

77. *Letters,* p 145 (28 Aug 1849).

78. *Speeches* 1, p 114 (6 Sep 1849).

79. Quoted from Schoeps, *Bismarck über Zeitgenossen – Zeitgenossen über Bismarck*, p 194.

80. *Speeches* 1, p 235.

81. Quoted from Marcks, *Bismarck. Eine Biographie*, p 520f.

82. *Speeches* 1, pp 264, 268.

83. *Letters,* p 266 (28 Apr 1851).

84. Ernst Ludwig von Gerlach, *Aufzeichnungen* Vol. 2, p 124.

85. *Letters,* p 281 (18 May 1851).

86. Arnold Oskar Meyer, *Bismarcks Kampf mit Österreich am Bundestag zu Frankfurt (1851–1859)* (Berlin–Leipzig: 1927) p 407, hereafter Meyer, *Bismarcks Kampf.*

87. As reported by Thun on 21 Sep 1851, Meyer, *Bismarcks Kampf,* p 44.

88. Bismarck to Manteuffel, referring to conversation with Thun, November 1851, *Works* 1, p 105.

89. Meyer, *Bismarcks Kampf,* p 71.

90. Bismarck to Leopold von Gerlach, 19/20 Dec 1853, *Works* 14, p 334.

91. As Bismarck said in November 1853, Keudell, p 43.

92. Andreas Kaernbach, *Bismarcks Konzept zur Reform des Deutschen Bundes. Zur Kontinuität der Politik Bismarcks und Preussens in der deutschen Frage* (Göttingen: 1991) p 68, hereafter Kaernbach, *Bismarcks Konzept zur Reform des Deutschen Bundes.*

93. Bismarck to Manteuffel, 15 Feb 1854, *Works* 1, p 427.

94. Bismarck to Manteuffel, 15 Feb 1854, *Works* 1, p 427.

95. According to Engelberg, *Bismarck* Vol. 1, p 429.

96. *Letters,* p 367 (27 Aug 1855).

97. Horst Kohl (ed.), *Briefe des Generals Leopold von Gerlach an Otto von Bismarck.* (Berlin: 1912) p 206.

98. Bismarck to Leopold von Gerlach, 2 May 1857, *Works* 14, p 465.

99. Memorandum of Bismarck to Prince Wilhelm, 30 Mar 1858, *Works* 2, pp 302–22.

100. Quoted from Kaernbach, *Bismarcks Konzept zur Reform des Deutschen Bundes,* p 110.

101. Bismarck to his sister, 10 Dec 1858, *Works* 14, p 495.

102. Keudell, p 69.

103. *Briefwechsel von John Lothrop Motley. Aus dem Englischen übersetzt von A. Eltze* Vol. 1, (Berlin: 1890) p 178.

104. *Letters,* p 412 (6 Apr 1859).

105. Kurd von Schlözer, Leopold von Schlözer (ed.), *Petersburger Briefe 1857–1862* (Stuttgart–Berlin: 1922) p 127.

106. Schlözer, *Petersburger Briefe,* p 156 (Oct 1860).

107. Schlözer, *Petersburger Briefe,* p 169 (26/14 Nov 1860).

108. Johanna von Bismarck to Robert von Keudell, 12 Aug 1859, Keudell, p 71f.

109. Johanna von Bismarck to Robert von Keudell, 30 Jan 1860, Keudell, p 75.

110. Roon, *Denkwürdigkeiten* Vol. 2, p 95 (Roon to Bismarck, 4 Jun 1862).

111. Roon, *Denkwürdigkeiten,* p 91 (Bismarck to Roon, 2 Jun 1862).

112. Carl Friedrich Vitzthum von Eckstädt, *St. Petersburg und London in den Jahren 1852–1864* Vol. 2 (Stuttgart: 1886) p 158.

113. *Letters,* p 500 (19 Aug 1862).

114. Johanna von Bismarck to Robert von Keudell, 7 Sep 1862, Keudell, p 96.

115. Prince Nikolai Orloff, *Bismarck und Katharina Orloff. Ein Idyll in der hohen Politik* (Munich: 1936) p 134.

116. Keudell, p 110.

117. Conversation in Babelsberg, 22 Sep 1862, *Works* 15, p 179 (the following quotation is from p 178).

118. Quoted from Otto Nirrnheim, *Das erste Jahr des Ministeriums Bismarck und die öffentliche Meinung* (Heidelberg: 1908) p 70.

119. Heinrich Abeken, *Ein schlichtes Leben in bewegter Zeit. Aus Briefen zusammengestellt* (3rd ed., Berlin: 1904) p 284.

120. Hellmut Diwald (ed. and introduction), *Von der Revolution zum Norddeutschen Bund. Politik und Ideengut der preußischen Hochkonservativen 1848–1866. Aus dem Nachlaß von Ernst Ludwig von Gerlach* Part 1: *Tagebuch 1848–1866* (Göttingen: 1970) p 435 (8 Oct 1862).

121. Schlözer, *Petersburger Briefe*, p 261 (5 Oct 1862).

122. *Speeches* 2, p 30.

123. Max Cornelius (ed.), *Heinrich von Treitschkes Briefe* (Leipzig: 1918) p 239 (19 Oct 1862), p 238 (29/30 Sep 1862).

124. *Works* 15, p 194f.

125. *Speeches* 2, p 81.

126. Quoted from Gall, *Bismarck. Der weiße Revolutionär*, p 279.

127. Quoted from Stern, *Gold und Eisen*, p 60.

128. Quoted from Pflanze, *Bismarck*, Vol. 1, p 208f.

129. Theodor Bernhardi in his diary, quoted from Pflanze, *Bismarck* Vol. 1, p 214.

130. Kaiser Friedrich III, Heinrich Otto Meisner (ed.), *Tagebücher von 1848–1866* (Leipzig: 1929) p 198 (5 Jun 1863).

131. Ernst Ludwig von Gerlach, *Aufzeichnungen* Vol. 2, p 249 (11 Nov 1862).

132. *Works* 11, p 606.

133. Bismarck to Motley, 17 Apr 1863, *Briefwechsel von J. L. Motley* Vol. 1, p 143f.

134. See above all Egmont Zechlin, *Bismarck und die Grundlegung der deutschen Großmacht* (1st ed.: 1930).

135. Bismarck to Graf Berstorff, 25/13 Nov 1861; *Works* 3, p 298f.

136. Perthes to Roon, 25 Feb and 4 Mar 1863, Roon, *Denkwürdigkeiten* Vol. 2, pp 137, 140.

137. J. Bindewald to Ludwig von Gerlach, 31 Aug 1863, *Von der Revolution zum Norddeutschen Bund* part 2 (Göttingen: 1970) p 1149.

138. *Works* 4, p 170; cf. Kaernbach, *Bismarcks Konzept zur Reform des Deutschen Bundes*, pp 194ff.

139. Quoted from Pflanze, *Bismarck* Vol. 1, p 188.

140. Keudell, p 140.

141. *Works* 14, p 659.

142. Quoted from Stern, *Gold und Eisen*, p 78.

143. Wilhelm von Kügelgen, Walter Killy (ed. and introduction), *Bürgerleben. Die Briefe an den Bruder Gerhard 1840–1867* (Munich: 1990) p 895.

144. Heinrich von Treitschke to Franz Overbeck, 7 May 1864, and to Salomon Hirzel, 19 May 1864, Heinrich von Treitschke, *Briefe* Vol. 2, pp 324, 326.

145. Bismarck to Robert Graf von der Goltz, 16 Aug 1865, *Works* 5, p 270.

146. Bismarck to Guido Graf von Usedom (envoy to Florence), 16 Aug 1865, *Works* 5, p 275.

147. Keudell, p 228.

148. Quoted from Engelberg, *Bismarck* Vol. 1, p 570.

149. *Works* 7, p 123.

150. Roon, *Denkwürdigkeiten* Vol. 2, p 400.

151. Quoted from Engelberg, *Bismarck* Vol. 1, p 574.

152. *Von der Revolution zum Norddeutschen Bund* part 2, p 1265f.

153. Quoted from Kraus, *Ernst Ludwig von Gerlach, Politisches Denken und Handeln eines preußischen Altkonservativen* part 1, p 805.

154. Rudolf von Delbrück, *Lebenserinnerungen 1817–1867* Vol. 2 (Leipzig: 1905) p 370.

155. Heinrich Sybel to Hermann Baumgarten, 14 May 1866, Julius Heyderhoff and Paul Wentzke (eds.), *Deutscher Liberalismus im Zeitalter Bismarcks. Eine politische Briefsammlung* Vol. 1 (Bonn: 1925) p 284.

156. Quoted from Pflanze, *Bismarck* Vol. 1, p 310.

157. Quoted from Gordon A Craig, *Königgrätz 1866. Eine Schlacht macht Weltgeschichte* (Vienna: 1997) p 10.

158. In conversation with the Hungarian Count Seherr-Thoss, 8 Jul 1866, *Works* 7, p 140.

159. *Letters*, p 572.

160. *Works* 15, p 277.

161. Quoted from Gall, *Bismarck. Der weiße Revolutionär*, p 376.

162. Rudolf von Ihering in *Briefen an seine Freunde* (Leipzig: 1913) p 196 (1 May 1866) and p 206 (19 Aug 1866).

163. Quoted from Heinrich August Winkler, *Preußischer Liberalismus und deutscher Nationalstaat. Studien zur Geschichte der Deutschen Fortschrittspartei 1861–1866* (Tübingen: 1964) p 110.

164. Rudolf Seyerlen (ed.), Johann Caspar Bluntschli, *Denkwürdigkeiten aus meinem Leben* Vol. 3 (Nördlingen: 1884) p 160.

165. Heinrich von Treitschke to Georg Reimer, 1 Dec 1866, Heinrich von Treitschke, *Briefe* Vol. 3 (Leipzig: 1920), p 103, note 1. On the problem of the 'revolution from above', cf. E. Engelberg, *Bismarck* Vol. 1, p 619–21; Gall, *Bismarck. Der weiße Revolutionär*, pp 380–3.

166. Bismarck to Lieutenant-General Freiherr von Manteuffel *Works* 6, p 120.

167. Perthes to Roon, 16 Apr 1866, Roon, *Denkwürdigkeiten*, Vol. 2, p 414.

168. *Works* 6, p 167.

169. Quoted from Gall, *Bismarck. Der weiße Revolutionär*, p 352.

170. Bismarck to his wife, 30 Jun 1867, *Works* 14, p 727.

171. Graf Alexander Keyserling, *Ein Lebensbild aus seine Briefen und Tagebüchern, zusammengestellt von Freifrau Helene von Taube von der Nissen* Vol. 1 (Berlin: 1902) p 549.

172. Cf. Ederhard Kolb, 'Großpreußen oder Kleindeutschland? Zu Bismarcks deutscher Politik im Reichsgründungsjahrzehnt' in Johannes Kunisch (ed.), *Bismarck und seine Zeit* (Berlin: 1992) p 34.

173. Bismarck in conversation with General-Quartermaster Suckow of Württemberg, 11 May 1868, *Works* 7, p 259.

174. Hans-Ulrich Wehler, *Deutsche Gesellschaftsgeschichte* Vol. 3: *Von der "Deutschen Doppelrevolution" bis zum Beginn des Ersten Weltkriegs 1849–1914* (Munich: 1995) p 311.

175. Quoted from Engelberg, *Bismarck* Vol. 1, p 679.

176. Memorandum to von Werthern, 26 Feb 1869, *Works* 6b, p 2.

177. *Works* 6a, p 412.

178. Among the extensive literature on the 'war guilt question' of 1870, cf. especially Eberhard Kolb, *Der Kriegsausbruch 1870. Politische Entscheidungsprozesse und Verantwortlichkeiten in der Julikrise 1870* (Göttingen: 1970); Josef Becker, 'Zum Problem der Bismarckschen Politik in der spanischen Thronfrage 1870', *Historische Zeitschrift* 212 (1971), pp 529–605, hereafter Becker, 'Zum Problem'; J. Becker, 'Von Bismarcks "spanischer Diversion" zur "Emser Legende" des Reichsgründers', in Johannes Burckhardt et al., *Lange und kurze Wege in den Ersten Weltkrieg* (Munich: 1996) pp 87–113, hereafter Becker, 'Von Bismarcks "spanischer Diversion"'. Cf. also the penetrating analysis in Hans-Ulrich Wehler, *Deutsche Gesellschaftsgeschichte*, Vol. 3, pp 319–22.

179. Quoted from Becker, 'Zum Problem', p 591.

180. Keudell, p 429.

181. Becker, 'Von Bismarcks "spanischer Diversion"', p 94.

182. Busch 1, p 294 (14 Oct 1870).

183. Busch 1, p 200 (16 Sep 1870).

184. Paul Bronsart von Schellendorf, Peter Rassow (ed.), *Geheimes Kriegstagebuch* (Bonn: 1954) p 311.

185. Quoted from Gall, *Bismarck. Der weiße Revolutionär*, p 442.

186. Walter Lipkens, 'Bismarck, die öffentliche Meinung und die Annexion von Elsaß und Lothringen 1870', *Historische Zeitschrift* 199 (1964) pp 31–112; for a contrary view see L. Gall, 'Zur Frage der Annexion von Elsaß und Lothringen 1870', *Historische Zeitschrift* 206 (1968) pp 265–326; later, Eberhard Kolb, *Der Weg aus dem Krieg. Bismarcks Politik im Krieg und die Friedensanbahnung 1870/1871* (Munich: 1989) pp 113 ff.

187. Memorandum to Albrecht Graf von Bernstorff, 21 Aug 1870, quoted from Kolb, *Der Weg aus dem Krieg*, p 160.

188. Busch 1, p 427.

189. Busch 2, p 60.

190. *Works* 14, p 810.

191. Busch 1, p 465.

192. Quoted from Klaus Hildebrand, *Das vergangene Reich. Deutsche Außenpolitik von Bismarck bis Hitler* (Stuttgart: 1995) p 30.

193. Cf. Andreas Hillgruber, 'Die "Krieg-in-Sicht"-Krise 1975' in Hillgruber, *Deutsche Großmacht- und Weltpolitik im 19. Und 20. Jahrhundert* (Düsseldorf: 1977) pp 35–52.

194. *Speeches* 6, p 461.

195. Quoted from Gregor Schöllgen, 'Zwischen Abstinenz und Engagement. Bismarck und die orientalische Frage' in Kunisch (ed.), *Bismarck und seine Zeit*, p 157.

196. Johannes Lepsius, Albrecht Mendelssohn-Bartholdy and Friedrich Thimme (eds.), *Die große Politik der europäischen Kabinette von 1871–1914. Sammlung der diplomatischen Akten des Auswärtigen Amtes* Vol. 2 (Berlin: 1922–7) p 154, hereafter *Die große Politik*.

197. Ulrich Noack, *Bismarcks Friedenspolitik und das Problem des deutschen Machtverfalls* (Leipzig: 1928) p 275; cf. Klaus

Hildebrand, '"System der Aushilfen"? Chancen und Grenzen deutscher Außenpolitik im Zeitalter Bismarcks (1871–1890)' in Kunisch (ed.), *Bismarck und seine Zeit*, pp 121–39.

198. *Speeches* 9, p 398.

199. Heinrich von Poschinger, *Fürst Bismarck und die Parlamentarier* Vol. 1: *Die Tischgespräche des Reichskanzlers* (Breslau: 1894) p 112.

200. Heinrich von Poschinger, *Fürst Bismarck und die Parlamentarier* Vol. 3: *1879–1890* (Breslau: 1896) p 54.

201. Cf. Wilfried Baumgart, 'Bismarcks Kolonialpolitik' in Kunisch (ed.), *Bismarck und seine Zeit*, pp 141–53.

202. Norman Rich and M. H. Fisher (eds.), *Die geheimen Papiere Friedrich von Holsteins* Vol. 2 (Berlin–Frankfurt am Main: 1957) p 174.

203. *Works* 8, p 646.

204. R. Lucius von Ballhausen, p 500 (17 Aug 1889).

205. Ludwig Bamberger, *Bismarck posthumus* (Berlin: 1899) p 8.

206. Cf. Hans-Ulrich Wehler, *Deutsche Gesellschaftsgeschichte* Vol. 3, pp 368ff; for a critical response, cf. Richard J. Evans, 'Bürgerliche Gesellschaft und charismatische Herrschaft', *Die Zeit* 42 (13 Oct 1995), literary supplement, pp 32f; John Breuilly, 'Auf dem Weg zur deutschen Gesellschaft? Der dritte Band von Wehlers "Gesellschaftsgeschichte"', in *Geschichte und Gesellschaft* 24 (1998), pp 136–68 (esp pp 154ff).

207. R. Lucius von Ballhausen, pp 21f (5 May 1872).

208. Cf. Stern, *Gold und Eisen*, pp 680ff.

209. *Speeches* 5, p 233.

210. Christoph von Tiedemann, *Sechs Jahre Chef der Reichskanzlei unter dem Fürsten Bismarck. Erinnerungen* (Leipzig: 1909) p 15 (25 Jan 1875).

211. Cf. the study by David Blackbourn, *Wenn ihr sie wiederseht, fragt wer sie sei. Marienerscheinungen in Marpingen – Aufstieg und Niedergang des deutschen Lourdes* (Reinbek bei Hamburg: 1997).

212. Michael Stürmer (ed.), *Bismarck und die preußisch-deutsche Politik 1871–1890* (Munich: 1970) p 125.

213. Quoted from Studt, *Lothar Bucher*, p 283.

214. *Speeches* 8, p 144.

215. Especially Helmut Böhme, *Deutschlands Weg zur Großmacht. Studien zum Verhältnis von Wirtschaft und Staat während der Reichsgründungszeit* (Cologne: 1966); for a contrary view, Engelberg, *Bismarck*, Vol. 2, p 319; Pflanze, *Bismarck* Vol. 2, pp 196ff.

216. Quoted from Wolfgang J. Mommsen, *Das Ringen um den nationalen Staat. Die Gr:undung und der innere Ausbau des Deutschen Reiches unter Otto von Bismarck 1850 bis 1890* (Berlin: 1993) p 567.

217. Freiherr von Mittnacht, *Erinnerungen an Bismarck. Neue Folge (1877–1889)* (Stuttgart–Berlin: 1905) p 42.

218. On this episode, cf. Erich Eyck, *Bismarck. Leben und Werk* Vol. 3 (Erlenbach–Zürich: 1944) p 378.

219. R. Lucius von Ballhausen, p 323 (29 Jan 1885).

220. Busch 3, p 17 (16 Nov 1885).

221. Orloff, *Bismarck und Katharina Orloff*, p 129.

222. Keudell, p 488.

223. R. Lucius von Ballhausen, p 21 (5 May 1872).

224. *Briefwechsel von John Lothrop Motley* Vol. 2, p 364 (25 Jul 1872). On Bismarck's illnesses, cf. particularly Pflanze, *Bismarck* Vol. 1, pp 564f.

225. Quoted from Pflanze, *Bismarck* Vol. 1, p 565f.

226. Tiedemann, *Sechs Jahre Chef der Reichskanzlei unter dem Fürsten Bismarck. Erinnerungen*, p 13 (25 Jan 1875).

227. Quoted from Krockow, p 277.

228. Heinrich von Poschinger (ed.), *Fürst Bismarck. Neue Tischgespräche und Interviews* Vol. 2 (Stuttgart-Leipzig: 1899) p 349.

229. R. Lucius von Ballhausen, p 78 (31 Oct 1875).

230. *Das Tagebuch der Baronin Spitzemberg*, p 218 (3 Apr 1885).

231. On the details, cf. Engelberg, *Bismarck* Vol. 2, pp 352ff.

232. Roon, *Denkwürdigkeiten* Vol. 3, p 159 (16 Jan 1870).

233. Gerhard Ebel (ed.), *Paul Graf von Hatzfeldt. Nachgelassene Papiere* Vol. 1 (Boppard am Rhein: 1976) p 657.

234. Bismarck to General von Albedyll, the chief of the military cabinet, 19 Dec 1887, *Die große Politik* Vol. 6, p 59.

235. Quoted from John C. G. Roehl, *Wilhelm II. Die Jugend eines Kaisers 1859–1888* (Munich: 1993) p 739.

236. John C. G. Roehl (ed.), *Philipp Eulenburgs Politische Korrespondenz* Vol. I (Boppard am Rhein: 1976) p 377.

237. R. Lucius von Ballhausen, p 509 (24 Jan 1890). Also for the following quotation.

238. Prussian Staatsministerium minutes, 2 Mar 1890, first published in Egmont Zechlin, *Staatsstreichpläne Bismarcks und Wilhelms II. 1890–1894* (Stuttgart-Berlin: 1929) pp 179–84.

239. Quoted from Margaret L. Anderson, *Windthorst. Zentrumspolitiker und Gegenspieler Bismarcks* (Düsseldorf: 1988) p 403.

240. Letter of resignation of 18 Mar 1890 in *Works* 6c, pp 435ff (quotation p 438).

241. Theodor Fontane to Georg Friedländer, 1 May 1890, *Fontanes Briefe in zwei Bänden. Ausgewählt und erläutert von Gotthard Erler* Vol. 2 (Berlin-Weimar: 1968) p 273.

242. Pourtalès to Holstein, 20 Mar 1890, *Die geheimen Papiere Friedrich von Holsteins* Vol. 3, p 295.

243. *Works* 15, p 531.

244. *Das Tagebuch der Baronin Spitemberg*, p 272 (21 Mar 1890).

245. *Das Tagebuch der Baronin Spitemberg*, p 281 (23 May 1890).

246. Cf. Manfed Hank, *Kanzler ohne Amt. Fürst Bismarck nach seiner Entlassung 1890–1898* (Munich: 1980) pp 73ff.

247. *Das Tagebuch der Baronin Spitemberg*, p 287 (5 Mar 1891).

248. Quoted from Hank, *Kanzler ohne Amt*, p 26.

249. In a conversation with Maximilian Harden, February 1891, *Works* 9, p 118.

250. On the details, cf. Hank, *Kanzler ohne Amt*, pp 217ff.

251. Interview with the editor of the *Neue Freie Presse*, 23 Jun 1892, *Works* 9, pp 214ff.

252. *Das Tagebuch der Baronin Spitemberg*, p 321.

253. *Das Tagebuch der Baronin Spitemberg*, p 353 (3 Mar 1897).

254. *Works* 14, p 1017.

255. Quoted from Hank, *Kanzler ohne Amt*, p 442.

256. Hank, *Kanzler ohne Amt*, p 437.

257. Quoted from Gall, *Bismarck. Der weiße Revolutionär*, p 722.

258. Alfred Kerr, Günther Rühle (ed.), *Wo liegt Berlin? Briefe aus der Reichshauptstadt 1895–1900* (Berlin: 1997) p 407 (4 Aug 1898).

259. *Works* 9, p 89.

260. Cf. Dirk Reinartz/Christian Graf von Krockow, *Bismarck. Vom Verrat der Denkmäler* (Göttingen: 1991) pp 26f.

261. *Works* 13, p 559.

262. Quoted from Engelberg, *Bismarck* Vol. 2, p 643.

263. In a conversation with the journalist Anton Memminger, 16 Aug 1890, Heinrich von Poschinger (ed.), *Fürst Bismarck. Neue Tischgesprache und Interviews* Vol. 2, p 357.

264. *Letters,* p 541 (20 Jul 1864).

265. Quoted from Meyer, *Bismarcks Glaube*, p 9f.

266. K. Scheffer, *Bismarck* (1919), quoted from Gall, *Bismarck. Der weiße Revolutionär*, p 439.

267. Speech to students, 1 Apr 1895, *Works* 13, p 558.

268. Hermann Oncken, *Rudolf von Bennigsen. Ein deutscher liberaler Politiker* Vol. 2 (Stuttgart–Leipzig: 1910) p 382.

269. *Works* 9, p 355.

270. Quoted from Hans Kohn, *Wege und Irrwege. Vom Geist des deutschen Bürgertums* (Düsseldorf: 1962) pp 198, 201.

271. Max Weber, Johannes Winckelmann (ed.), *Gesammelte politische Schriften* 2nd expanded edition (Tübingen: 1958) pp 301, 303, 307.

272. Quoted from Hans-Günter Zmarzlik, *Das Bismarckbild der Deutschen – gestern und heute* (Freiburg: 1967) p 28.

273. Bamberger, *Bismarck posthumus*, p 63f.

274. Zmarzlik, *Das Bismarckbild der Deutschen*, p 8.

275. *Denkwürdigkeiten des Botschaftlers General von Schweinitz* Vol. 2 (Berlin: 1927) p 313.

276. Gall, *Bismarck. Der weiße Revolutionär*, p 725.

277. Willms, *Bismarck – Dämon der Deutschen*, pp 265, 347.

278. Krockow, p 8.

Chronology

1859	44	Envoy in St Petersburg.
1862	47	Envoy in Paris; flirtation with Katharina Orloff in Biarritz; 23 September: appointed Prussian prime minister; beginning of the struggle against the liberal opposition in the Prussian parliament; 30 September: 'Blood and iron' speech before the Budget Commission.
1863	48	Alvensleben Convention; discussions with Lassalle; rejects the participation of Prussia in the 'Princes' Diet' in Frankfurt.
1864	49	War between Prussia and Austria and Denmark.
1865	50	Gastein Convention.
1866	51	7 May: attempt on Bismarck's life on Unter den Linden; war between allies Prussia and Italy and Austria (and other states of the German Confederation); 3 July: victory at Königgrätz; preliminary peace of Nikolsburg; resolution of the constitutional conflict (Indemnity Bill).
1867	52	Sale of the estate of Varzin in Pomerania. Foundation and development of the North German Federation (Bismarck is Federal Chancellor). Luxemburg Crisis.
1868	53	Elections to Customs Parliament.
1870	55	Hohenzollern candidacy to the Spanish throne; 'Emser Depesche' and outbreak of the Franco-Prussian War; 2 September: victory at Sedan; investment of Paris; treaties with the southern German states to found the German Reich.
1871	56	18 January: Imperial Proclamation at Versailles; Bismarck made a prince; receives the Sachsenwald as a present; peace treaty with France

1872	57	Beginning of the 'Kulturkampf' against the Catholics: Jesuits expelled from Germany.
1873	58	Three Emperors' Agreement between Wilhelm I, Franz Joseph I of Austria-Hungary, and Tsar Alexander II.
1874	59	13 July: attempt on Bismarck's life in Bad Kissingen.
1875	60	'War in sight' crisis.
1878	63	Attempts on the life of Wilhelm I; break with the liberals and 'Socialist Laws'; Congress of Berlin.
1879	64	Dual Alliance with Austria-Hungary; passing of the protective tariff laws.
1881	66	Three Emperors' Treaty between the German Reich, Austria-Hungary, and Russia (renewed in 1884).
1882	67	Triple Alliance between the German Reich, Austria-Hungary, and Italy.
1883	68	Beginning of social legislation: health insurance (1884: accident insurance; 1889: disability insurance and old age pensions).
1884	69	Acquisition of German colonies in South-West Africa.
1885	70	Congo Conference in Berlin.
1887	72	Reinsurance Treaty with Russia.
1888	73	Year of three Kaisers: death of Wilhelm I, ninety-nine-day reign of Friedrich III, ascension to the throne of Wilhelm II.
1890	75	Break between Bismarck and Wilhelm II; 20 March: dismissed by the Kaiser.
1892	77	Visit to Vienna.
1894	79	Official reconciliation with Wilhelm II; death of Johanna.
1895	80	Eightieth birthday: the Reichstag refuses to send a congratulatory address.

| 1896 | 81 | The *Hamburger Nachrichten* reveal details of the Reinsurance Treaty. |
| 1898 | 83 | 30 July: Bismarck dies. |

Bibliography

1. Bibliographies, literature surveys, reference works

Bedürftig, Friedemann, *Taschenlexikon Bismarck* (Munich: 1998).

Born, Karl Erich (ed.), *Bismarck-Bibliographie. Quellen und Literatur zur Geschichte Bismarcks und seiner Zeit*, revised by Willy Hertel in collaboration with Hansjoachim Henning (Cologne–Berlin: 1966).

Gall, Lothar (ed.), *Das Bismarck-Problem in der Geschichtsschreibung nach 1945* (Cologne–Berlin: 1971).

Grützner, Friedhelm, *Die Politik Bismarcks 1862 bis 1871 in der deutschen Geschichtsschreibung. Eine kritische historiographische Betrachtung* (Frankfurt am Main–Bern–New York: 1986).

Halimann, Hans (ed.), *Revision des Bismarckbildes. Die Diskussion der deutschen Fachhistoriker 1945–1955* (Darmstadt: 1972).

Stolberg-Wernigerode, Albrecht Graf zu, *Bismarck-Lexikon. Quellenverzeichnis zu den in seinen Akten, Briefen, Gesprächen und Reden enthaltenen Äußerungen Bismarcks* (Stuttgart–Berlin: 1936).

Zmarzlik, Hans-Günter, *Das Bismarckbild der Deutschen - gestern und heute* (Freiburg: 1967).

2. Works

(a) Editions of works

Bismarck, Otto von, *Die gesammelten Werke. (Friedrichsruher Ausgabe)* 15 vols (Berlin: 1924–35).

——, Gustav Adolf Rein et al (eds.), *Werke in Auswahl.*
Jahrhundert-Ausgabe zum 23. September 1862. 4 parts in 8 vols
(Darmstadt: 1962–80).

(b) Speeches, letters, memoirs, conversations

Bismarck, Herbert Fürst von (ed.), *Fürst Bismarcks Briefe an seine*
Braut und Gattin (Stuttgart: 1900).

Bismarck, Otto von, Hanno Helbling (ed.), *Aus seinen Schriften,*
Briefen und Reden (Zurich: 1998).

——, *Briefe. Ausgewählt und eingeleitet von Hans Rothfels*
(Göttingen: 1955).

——, *Gedanken und Erinnerungen,* with an Essay by Lothar Gall
(Berlin: 1990).

——, Willy Andreas (ed.), *Gespräche* 3 vols (Bremen: 1963–5).

Gall, Lothar (ed.), *Bismarck. Die grossen Reden* (Berlin: 1981).

Kohl, Horst (ed.), *Bismarcks Briefe an General Leopold von Gerlach*
(Berlin: 1896).

—— (ed.), *Briefe Otto von Bismarcks an Schwester und Schwager*
1843–1897 (Leipzig: 1915).

—— (ed.), *Die politischen Reden des Fürsten Bismarck 1847–1897.*
Historisch-kritische Gesamtausgabe 14 vols (Stuttgart: 1892–
1905; reprint Aalen: 1969/70).

Petersdorff, Hermann von (ed.), *Bismarcks Briefwechsel mit Kleist-*
Retzow (Stuttgart–Berlin: 1919).

Poschinger, Heinrich von (ed.), *Fürst Bismarck und die*
Parlamentarier 3 vols (Breslau: 1894–6).

—— (ed.), *Fürst Bismarck. Neue Tischgespräche und Interviews*
2 vols (Stuttgart–Leipzig–Berlin–Vienna: 1895–9).

Raschdau, Ludwig (ed.), *Die politischen Berichte des Fürsten*
Bismarck aus Petersburg und Paris (1859–1862) 2 vols (Berlin:
1920).

Sempell, Charlotte, 'Unbekannte Briefstellen Bismarcks',
Historische Zeitschrift 207 (1968) pp 609–16).

Zeising, A. (ed.), *Briefwechsel Otto von Bismarcks mit Gustav
Scharlach* (Weimar: 1912).

3. Biographies, historical overviews

Bussmann, Walter, *Das Zeitalter Bismarcks* (Konstanz: 1956).

Craig, Gordon A., *Deutsche Geschichte 1866–1945. Vom
Norddeutschen Bund bis zum Ende des Dritten Reiches* (Munich:
1980).

Engelberg, Ernst, *Bismarck* Vol. 1: *Urpreuße und Reichsgründer*;
Vol. 2: *Das Reich in der Mitte Europas* (Berlin: 1985/90).

Engelberg, Waltraut, *Otto und Johanna von Bismarck* (Berlin:
1990).

——, *Das private Leben der Bismarcks* (Berlin: 1998).

Eyck, Erich, *Bismarck. Leben und Werk* 3 vols (Erlenbach–Zurich:
1941–4).

Gall, Lothar, *Bismarck. Der weiße Revolutionär* (Frankfurt am
Main–Berlin–Vienna: 1980 (paperback ed., 1983)).

——, *Bismarck. Ein Lebensbild* (Bergisch Gladbach: 1991).

Herre, Franz, *Bismarck. Der preußische Deutsche* (Cologne: 1991).

Hillgruber, Andreas, *Otto von Bismarck. Gründer der europäischen
Großmacht Deutsches Reich* (Göttingen–Zurich–Frankfurt am
Main: 1978).

Krockow, Christian Graf von, *Bismarck* (Stuttgart: 1997).

Ludwig, Emil, *Bismarck. Geschichte eines Kämpfers* (Berlin: 1926).

Marcks, Erich, *Bismarck. Eine Biographie 1815–1851* (Stuttgart-
Berlin: 1939).

Meyer, Arnold Oskar, *Bismarck. Der Mensch und der Staatsmann*
(2nd ed. Stuttgart: 1949).

Mommsen, Wilhelm, *Bismarck. Ein politisches Lebensbild*
(Munich: 1959).

Mommsen, Wolfgang J., *Das Ringen um den nationalen Staat. Die Gründung und der innere Ausbau des Deutschen Reiches unter Otto von Bismarck 1850 bis 1890* (Berlin: 1993).

Nipperdey, Thomas, *Deutsche Geschichte 1800–1866. Bürgerwelt und starker Staat* (Munich: 1983).

——, *Deutsche Geschichte 1866–1918*. Vol. 2: *Machtstaat vor der Demokratie* (Munich: 1992).

Opitz, Eckardt, *Die Bismarcks in Friedrichsruh* (Hamburg: 1990).

Palmer, Alan, *Bismarck. Eine Biographie* (Düsseldorf: 1976; Bergisch Gladbach: 1989).

Pflanze, Otto, *Bismarck* Vol. 1: *Der Reichsgründer*; Vol. 2: *Der Reichskanzler* (Munich: 1997/98).

Richter, Werner, *Bismarck* (Frankfurt am Main: 1962; 2nd ed. 1971).

Stürmer, Michael, *Das ruhelose Reich. Deutschland 1866–1918* (Berlin: 1983).

Ullrich, Volker, *Die nervöse Großmacht. Aufstieg und Untergang des deutschen Kaiserreichs 1871–1918* (Frankfurt am Main: 1997).

Wehler, Hans-Ulrich, *Deutsche Gesellschaftsgeschichte* Vol. 3: *Von der 'Deutschen Doppelrevolution' bis zum Beginn des Ersten Weltkrieges 1849–1914* (Munich: 1995).

Willms, Johannes, *Bismarck – Dämon der Deutschen. Anmerkungen zu einer Legende* (Munich: 1997).

4. Bismarck and his contemporaries: memoirs, letters, diaries, portraits

Abeken, Heinrich, *Ein schlichtes Leben in bewegter Zeit. Aus Briefen zusammengestellt* (3rd enlarged ed. Berlin: 1904).

Anderson, Margaret L., *Windthorst. Zentrumspolitiker und Gegenspieler Bismarcks* (Düsseldorf: 1988).

Bamberger, Ludwig, Ernst Feder (ed.), *Bismarcks großes Spiel. Die* geheimen *Tagebücher Ludwig Bambergers* (Frankfurt am Main: 1932).

Beust, Friedrich-Ferdinand Graf von, *Aus drei Viertel-Jahrhunderten. Erinnerungen und Aufzeichnungen.* 2 vols (Stuttgart: 1887).

Bismarck, Herbert Graf von, Walter Bussmann (ed.), *Aus seiner politischen Privatkorrespondenz* (Göttingen: 1964).

Bronsart von Schellendorf, Paul, *Geheimes Kriegstagebuch 1870–1871* (Bonn: 1954).

Busch, Moritz, *Tagebuchblätter* 3 vols (Leipzig: 1899).

Craig, Gordon A., *Über Fontane* (Munich: 1997).

Delbrück, Rudolf von, *Lebenserinnerungen 1817–1867* 2 vols (Leipzig: 1905).

Diwald, Hellmut (ed.), *Von der Revolution zum Norddeutschen Bund. Politik und Ideengut der preußischen Hochkonservativen 1848–1866. Aus dem Nachlaß von Ernst Ludwig von Gerlach* 2 parts (Göttingen: 1970).

Fontane, Theodor, *Briefe in zwei Bänden. Ausgewählt und erläutert von Gotthard Erlen* (Berlin and Weimar: 1968).

Fuchs, Walter Peter (ed.), *Großherzog Friedrich I. von Baden und die Reichspolitik 1871–1907* 2 vols (Stuttgart: 1968/75).

Gerlach, Ernst Ludwig von, Jakob von Gerlach (ed.), *Aufzeichnungen aus seinem Leben und Wirken 1795–1877* (Schwerin: 1903).

Gerlach, Leopold von, *Denkwürdigkeiten aus dem Leben Leopold von Gerlachs. Nach seinen Aufzeichnungen hg. von seiner Tochter* 2 vols (Berlin: 1891/92).

Hatzfeldt, Paul Graf von, Gerhard Ebel and Michael Behnen (eds.), *Nachgelassene Papiere* 2 vols (Boppard: 1976).

Holborn, Hajo (ed.), *Aufzeichnungen und Erinnerungen aus dem Leben des Botschafters Joseph Maria von Radowitz* 2 vols (Berlin and Leipzig: 1925).

Holstein, Friedrich von, Norman Rich and M. H. Fisher
(eds.), *Die geheimen Papiere Friedrich von Holsteins* 4 vols
(Göttingen–Berlin–Frankfurt am Main: 1956–63).

Ihering, Rudolf von, *Briefe an seine Freunde* (Leipzig: 1913).

Kerr, Alfred, Günther Rühle (ed.), *Wo liegt Berlin? Briefe aus der
Reichshauptstadt 1895–1900* (Berlin: 1997).

Keudell, Robert von, *Fürst und Fürstin Bismarck. Erinnerungen
aus den Jahren 1846 bis 1872* (Berlin–Stuttgart: 1901).

Keyserling, Graf Alexander, *Ein Lebensbild aus seinen Briefen
und Tagebüchern. Zusammengestellt von seiner Tochter Freifrau
Helene von Taube von der Issen* 2 vols (Berlin: 1902).

Kraus, Hans-Christof, *Ernst Ludwig von Gerlach. Politisches
Denken und Handeln eines preußischen Altkonservativen* 2 vols
(Göttingen: 1994).

Kügelgen, Wilhelm von, Walter Killy (ed.), *Bürgerleben. Die Briefe
an den Bruder Gerhard 1840–1867* (Munich: 1990).

Lucius von Ballhausen, Robert Freiherr, *Bismarck-Erinnerungen*
(Stuttgart–Berlin: 1920).

Meisner, Heinrich Otto (ed.), *Kaiser Friedrich III: Tagebücher
1848 bis 1866* (Leipzig: 1929).

Motley, John Lothrop, *Briefwechsel. Aus dem Englischen übersetzt
von A. Eltze* 2 vols (Berlin: 1890).

Oncken, Hermann, *Rudolf von Bennigsen. Ein deutscher liberaler
Politiker nach seinen Briefen und hinterlassenen Papieren* 2 vols
(Stuttgart–Leipzig: 1910).

Orloff, Nicolai Fürst, *Bismarck und die Fürstin Orloff. Ein Idyll in
der hohen Politik* (Munich: 1936).

Poschinger, Heinrich von, *Aus großer Zeit. Erinnerungen an den
Fürsten Bismarck* (Berlin: 1905).

Roehl, John C. G., *Wilhelm II. Die Jugend eines Kaisers 1859–1888*
(Munich: 1993),

——, *Wilhelm II. Der Aufbau der Persönlichen Monarchie 1888–1900* (Munich: 2001).

Roon, Albrecht Graf von, *Denkwürdigkeiten aus dem Leben des Generalfeldmarschalls Kriegsministers Grafen von Roon* 3 vols (5th ed. Berlin: 1905).

Schlözer, Kurd von, Leopold von Schlözer (ed.), *Petersburger Briefe 1857–1862* (Stuttgart–Berlin: 1922).

Schoeps, Hans-Joachim, *Bismarck über Zeitgenossen - Zeitgenossen über Bismarck* (Frankfurt am Main–Berlin–Vienna: 1972 (paperback ed., 1981)).

Schweinitz, Hans Lothar von, Wilhelm von Schweinitz (ed.), *Denkwürdigkeiten des Botschafters General von Schweinitz* 2 vols (Berlin: 1927).

Stern, Fritz, *Gold und Eisen. Bismarck und sein Bankier Bleichröder* (Frankfurt am Main–Berlin: 1978; paperback ed., Reinbek bei Hamburg: 1988).

Studt, Christoph, *Lothar Bucher (1817–1892). Ein politisches Leben zwischen Revolution und Staatsdienst* (Göttingen: 1992).

Tiedemann, Christoph von, *Sechs Jahre Chef der Reichskanzlei unter dem Fürsten Bismarck. Erinnerungen* (Leipzig: 1909).

Treitschke, Heinrich von, Max Cornicelius (ed.), *Briefe* 2 vols (Leipzig: 1913).

Vierhaus, Rudolf (ed.), *Das Tagebuch der Baronin Spitzemberg. Aufzeichnungen aus der Hofgesellschaft des Hohenzollernreiches* (Göttingen: 1960 (5th ed. 1989)).

Weber, Marie-Lise, *Ludwig Bamberger. Ideologie statt Realpolitik* (Stuttgart: 1987).

Wentzcke, Paul, and Julius Heyderhoff, *Deutscher Liberalismus im Zeitalter Bismarcks. Eine politische Briefsammlung* 2 vols (Bonn: 1925/26; reprint Osnabrück: 1970).

Windthorst, Ludwig, Hans-Georg Aschoff and Heinz-Jörg

Heinrich (eds.), *Briefe* Vol. 1: 1834–1888; Vol. 2: 1881–1891 (Paderborn: 1994/2002).

5. Essay collections, monographs

Afflerbach, Holger, *Der Dreibund. Europäische Großmacht- und Allianzpolitik vor dem Ersten Weltkrieg* (Vienna–Cologne–Weimar: 2002).

Aretin, Karl Otmar Freiherr von (ed.), *Bismarcks Außenpolitik und der Berliner Kongreß* (Wiesbaden: 1978).

Biefang, Andreas, *Bismarcks Reichstag. Das Parlament in der Leipziger Straße. Fotografiert von Julius Braatz* (Düsseldorf: 2002).

Böhme, Helmut, *Deutschlands Weg zur Großmacht. Studien zum Verhältnis von Wirtschaft und Staat während der Reichsgründungszeit* (Cologne: 1966).

Craig, Gordon A., *Königgrätz. 1866 – Eine Schlacht macht Weltgeschichte* (Vienna: 1997).

Dülffer, Jost, and Hans Hübner, *Otto von Bismarck. Person – Politik – Mythos* (Berlin: 1993).

Elzer, Herbert, *Bismarcks Bündnispolitik von 1887. Erfolg und Grenzen einer europäischen Friedensordnung* (Frankfurt am Main: 1991).

Gall, Lothar (ed.), *Otto von Bismarck und Wilhelm II. Repräsentanten eines Epochenwechsels?* (Paderborn: 2000).

—— (ed.), *Otto von Bismarck und die Parteien* (Paderborn: 2001).

Goldberg, Hans-Peter, *Bismarck und seine Gegner. Die politische Rhetorik im kaiserlichen Reichstag* (Düsseldorf: 1998).

Hachtmann, Rüdiger, *Berlin 1848. Eine Politik- und Gesellschaftsgeschichte der Revolution* (Bonn: 1997).

Hampe, Karl-Alexander, *Das Auswärtige Amt in der Ära Bismarck* (Bonn: 1995).

Hank, Manfred, *Kanzler ohne Amt. Fürst Bismarck nach seiner Entlassung 1890–1898* (Munich: 1980).

Hildebrand, Klaus, *Das vergangene Reich. Deutsche Außenpolitik von Bismarck bis Hitler* (Stuttgart: 1995).

——, *No intervention. Die Pax Britannica und Preußen 1865/66–1869/70* (Munich: 1997).

Hillgruber, Andreas, *Deutsche Großmacht- und Weltpolitik im 19. und 20. Jahrhundert* (Düsseldorf: 1977).

Kaernbach, Andreas, *Bismarcks Konzept zur Reform des Deutschen Bundes. Zur Kontinuität der Politik Bismarcks und Preußens in der deutschen Frage* (Göttingen: 1991).

Kolb, Eberhard, *Der Kriegsausbruch 1870. Politische Entscheidungsprozesse und Verantwortlichkeiten in der Julikrise 1870* (Göttingen: 1970).

——, *Der Weg aus dem Krieg. Bismarcks Politik im Krieg und die Friedensanbahnung 1870/71* (Munich: 1989).

—— (ed.), *Europa und die Reichsgründung. Preußen-Deutschland in der Sicht der großen europäischen Mächte 1860–1880* (Munich: 1980).

Kunisch, Johannes (ed.), *Bismarck und seine Zeit* (Berlin: 1992).

Lappenküper, Ulrich, *Die Mission Radowitz. Untersuchungen zur Rußlandpolitik Otto von Bismarcks (1871–1875)* (Göttingen: 1990).

Machtan, Lothar (ed.), *Bismarcks Sozialstaat. Beiträge zur Geschichte der Sozialpolitik und zur sozialpolitischen Geschichtsschreibung* (Frankfurt am Main–New York: 1994).

—— (ed.), *Bismarck und der deutsche Nationalmythos* (Bremen: 1994).

——, *Bismarcks Tod und Deutschlands Tränen. Reportage einer Tragödie* (Munich: 1998).

Mayer, Gustav, *Bismarck und Lassalle. Ihr Briefwechsel und ihre Gespräche* (Berlin: 1928).

Meyer, Arnold Oskar, *Bismarcks Kampf mit Österreich am Bundestag zu Frankfurt (1851 bis 1859)* (Berlin–Leipzig: 1927).

——,*Bismarcks Glaube im Spiegel der "Loosungen und Lehrtexte"* (Munich: 1933).

Mommsen, Wolfgang J., *Der autoritäre Nationalstaat. Verfassung, Gesellschaft und Kultur des deutschen Kaiserreichs* (Frankfurt am Main: 1990).

Müller-Link, Horst, *Industrialisierung und Außenpolitik. Preußen-Deutschland und das Zarenreich 1860–1890* (Göttingen: 1977).

Münche, Fritz, *Bismarcks Affäre Arnim. Die Politik des Diplomaten und die Verantwortlichkeit des Staatsmanns* (Berlin: 1990).

Naujoks, Eberhard, *Bismarcks auswärtige Pressepolitik und die Reichsgründung (1865–1871)* (Wiesbaden: 1968).

Nirrnheim, Otto, *Das erste Jahr des Ministeriums Bismarck und die öffentliche Meinung* (Heidelberg: 1908).

Nissen, Walter, *Otto von Bismarcks Göttinger Studentenjahre 1832–1833* (Göttingen: 1982).

Noack, Ulrich, *Bismarcks Friedenspolitik und das Problem des deutschen Machtverfalls* (Leipzig: 1928).

Noell von der Nahmer, Robert, *Bismarcks Reptilienfonds. Aus den Geheimakten Preußens und des Deutschen Reiches* (Mainz: 1968).

Parr, Rolf, *"Zwei Seelen wohnen, ach! in meiner Brust!" Strukturen und Funktionen der Mythisierung Bismarcks* (Munich: 1992).

Pöls,Werner, *Sozialistenfrage und Revolutionsfurcht in ihrem Zusammenhang mit angeblichen Staatsstreichplänen Bismarcks* (Hamburg–Lübeck: 1960).

Reinartz, Dirk, and Christian Graf von Krockow, *Bismarck. Vom Verrat der Denkmäler* (Göttingen: 1991).

Rosenberg, Hans, *Große Depression und Bismarckzeit. Wirtschaftsablauf, Gesellschaft und Politik in Mitteleuropa* (Berlin: 1967).

Schaefer, Jürgen W., *Kanzlerbild und Kanzlermythos in der Zeit des "Neuen Kurses"* (Paderborn: 1973).

Scheuer, Friedrich, *Adler und Halbmond. Bismarck und der Orient 1878 bis 1890* (Paderborn: 2001).

Schieder, Theodor, and Ernst Deuerlein, *Reichsgründung 1870/71. Tatsachen, Kontroversen, Interpretationen* (Stuttgart: 1970).

Schoeps, Julius H., *Bismarck und sein Attentäter. Der Revolveranschlag Unter den Linden am 7 Mai 1866* (Frankfurt am Main–Berlin: 1984).

Stalman, Volker, *Die Partei Bismarcks. Die Deutsche Reichs- und Freikonservative Partei 1866–1890* (Düsseldorf: 2000).

Studt, Christoph, *Das Bismarckbild der deutschen Öffentlichkeit (1898–1998)* (Friedrichsruh: 1999).

Stunner, Michael, *Regierung und Reichstag im Bismarckstaat 1871–1880* (Düsseldorf: 1974).

——, *Die Reichsgründung. Deutscher Nationalstaat und europäisches Gleichgewicht im Zeitalter Bismarcks* (Munich: 1984).

Ullrich, Volker, *Fünf Schüsse auf Bismarck. Historische Reportagen* (Munich: 2002).

Wehler, Hans-Ulrich, *Bismarck und der Imperialismus* (4th ed. Munich: 1976).

Winkler, Heinrich August, *Preußischer Liberalismus und deutscher Nationalstaat. Studien zur Geschichte der Deutschen Fortschrittspartei* (Tübingen: 1964).

Zechlin, Egmont, *Staatsstreichpläne unter Bismarck und Wilhelm II. 1890–1894* (Stuttgart–Berlin: 1929).

——, *Bismarck und die Grundlegung der deutschen Großmacht* (2nd ed. Darmstadt: 1960).

Picture Sources

The author and publishers wish to express their thanks to the following sources of illustrative material and/or permission to reproduce it. They will make proper acknowledgments in future editions in the event that any omissions have occurred.

akg-Images: p. 59; Bismarck Museum: pp. 10, 89, 99; Getty Images: p. 86; all other pictures private collections or public domain.

Index